Windows on science and faith

'But this is just a simplistic way of looking at the problem.'

Windows on science and faith

Tim Hawthorne

Inter-Varsity Press

INTER-VARSITY PRESS
38 De Montfort Street, Leicester LE1 7GP, England

Unless otherwise stated, quotations from the Bible are taken from the
HOLY BIBLE: NEW INTERNATIONAL VERSION, © 1978 by
the International Bible Society, New York. Published in Great Britain
by Hodder and Stoughton Ltd., and used by permission of Zondervan
Bible Publishers, Grand Rapids, Michigan.

First published 1986

British Library Cataloguing in Publication Data

Hawthorne, J. N.
  Windows on science and faith.
  1. Religion and science.
  I. Title
  261.5'5   BL240.2

  ISBN 0–85110–447–9

Phototypeset in Linotron Ehrhardt
Typeset in Great Britain by Input Typesetting Ltd, London SW19 8DR
Printed and bound in Great Britain by
Cox & Wyman Ltd, Reading

*Inter-Varsity Press is the publishing division of the Universities and Colleges
Christian Fellowship (formerly the Inter-Varsity Fellowship), a student movement
linking Christian Unions in universities and colleges throughout the United
Kingdom and the Republic of Ireland, and a member movement of the International Fellowship of Evangelical Students. For information about local and
national activities write to UCCF, 38 De Montfort Street, Leicester LE1 7GP.*

Contents

Preface

I wrote a small book called *Questions of science and faith* in 1960. This is an almost complete re-write, since many things look different twenty-six years later. The book is intended for students and I have tried to make it intelligible to non-scientists as well as scientists. My aim is to show that being a Christian in a science-oriented culture doesn't involve intellectual suicide. I have had to deal therefore, with many fields of science, let alone philosophy and theology, for which I am not qualified. Brevity itself can sometimes give the wrong impression. I hope that there are not too many misrepresentations.

From students' letters and conversations I know that evolution still causes problems, so extra space has been devoted to it. Perhaps it is more important to be 'in love and charity' with our Christian neighbours who differ from us, than to adopt any particular position.

For those seriously interested in the subject this can only be an introductory text, so I have included a list of books for further reading, with my own feelings about each.

The cartoons appearing on the half-title page and on pages 35, 48, 94 and 114 are © Sidney Harris of Norwalk, Connecticut, and that on page 75 © Michael Gruber of Reston, Virginia.

I am grateful to them both for permission to reproduce these drawings.

My thanks are also due to Jenny Paxton for her patience, skill and speed in converting my scribble into a presentable typescript.

J. N. H.

1

Warfare?

A century ago it was popular to talk about the warfare between science and Christian belief. Andrew White, one of the founders of Cornell University, wrote a distinctly one-sided account of the conflict.[1] In it he pictured the noble army of science with its banners of light and truth fighting against the dark hordes of dogmatic theology, blinded by prejudice and resistant to progress.

Things look different today. Light, truth and noble sentiments do not immediately spring to mind in connection with science. Power, yes – perhaps too great for us to control. We all live in the shadow of that mushroom-shaped cloud which rose over the city of Hiroshima. After two disastrous world wars the old talk of human progress sounds hollow. Young people react against scientific technology because it helps the military machines of the great powers and supra-national industrial giants, concerned more about profits than people. Science for them is typified by defoliating agents, toxic wastes in rivers, silicon chips making workers redundant, drugs to control the mind and the prospect of genetic engineering: 1984 with a vengeance!

But we cannot escape from history. Is there less discussion of the conflict between science and faith nowadays because for many people science has won? The church, which persecuted Galileo because he showed that the earth moved round the sun, finally had to accept Galileo's science. Modern astronomy seems to make the earth even less significant, a mere speck in the vastness of a universe with countless millions of planets like it. The six days of creation in the book of Genesis seem to belong to a different world.

Or do they? In fact the Genesis account of creation has more to do with today's science than most people realize. The ancient Chinese had a respectable science and the Greeks might have done a great deal if philosophy had not got the better of them. As it was, experimental science as we know it did not blossom until the sixteenth century and it is no accident that it grew up in the Christian culture of Western Europe. Experimenting is a sort of manual labour and the Greek philosophers had looked down on manual work. The Bible, on the other hand, regards labour as honourable. Adam was directed to dress and keep the garden of Eden and Jesus himself was a carpenter. Even more important was the Jewish-Christian view of Nature. For the Hindu or Buddhist the material world has no value and his aim is to escape from the chain of existence into Nirvana where the soul is absorbed into the ultimate. For the Jew and the Christian things are very different. God is the creator of the heavens and the earth and at each stage of the creation account in the first chapter of Genesis comes the phrase 'God saw that it was good'. The sixteenth-century pioneers saw science as the study of God's handiwork and, encouraged by Francis Bacon, as a proper response to the biblical command to 'subdue the earth'.[2] For Kepler the heavens declared the glory of God and there was no conflict between science and faith. Newton wrote theological as well as scientific works. How strange then, that for many people today, this same science seems to leave no room for God.

The blind eye

E. F. Schumacher, of *Small is Beautiful* fame, described in another book[3] his experience with a map of Leningrad. He could see several large churches but there was no trace of them on the map. On asking an interpreter, he was told that churches were not shown on the official maps. Contradicting him, Schumacher pointed to one that was clearly marked. 'This is a museum', said the guide, 'not what we call a "living church". It is only the "living churches" we don't show.'

Russian communists are not alone in turning a blind eye to Christianity. For many of our teachers in schools and universities, for influential journalists and T.V. writers, the real world is mapped out by a science which ignores God. Jesus is an impressive figure to many of them, but the biblical claims that he was the Son of God, that he performed miracles and rose from the dead just do not fit in with their views of reality. Are they right? Does modern science make it impossible to accept the Christian faith? Or, in spite of everything, does it make more sense to believe that this incredible universe has a Designer who still cares for it, than to consider it a gigantic accident, and life a tale told by an idiot, signifying nothing? These are the questions for the chapters which follow, but before we move on, another question concerns us more closely.

Most biologists accept the theory of evolution in which all the present forms of life, including man, have developed from a common ancestor. Every species seems beautifully adapted to the environment in which it lives and this is an important feature of the theory. Every species except *homo sapiens* that is, for man seems to be out of control. None of the others slaughter one another on such a massive scale, nor do they have such power to change the world – and usually to be unhappy about the change. As Mark Twain said, 'Man is the only animal that blushes. Or needs to'. It is argued that Darwin's biology works well enough for the

11

other creatures. What went wrong with us? We are certainly special. The other apes do not write poetry or worry about the origin of life or pack themselves off to the moon. Special but spoilt. Would that be a fair assessment of the human predicament? I think so, but it's not original. It comes straight out of that creation account in Genesis about which people are still arguing. We shall meet it again.

2

Science

2

Science impresses us all. From weather satellites to wonder drugs, its achievements dominate our lives. But it is possible to be over-impressed, to assume that scientific truth is all that matters. 'These are the facts', we say, 'verifiable by experiment. Other so-called truth is subjective'.

What is science then? The word comes from the Latin for knowledge, but nowadays it means the study of nature, natural science. Its method relies on observation and experiment, on sitting down humbly before the facts like a little child, as T. H. Huxley put it. Having gathered those observations, the scientist draws out a theory from them, by a process of induction. If further experiments support the theory it becomes a 'law of science'. Or so it is often described, but the real process is usually rather different. Something akin to the inspiration of an artist may help the scientist to make sense of his observations. Sometimes it is even a dream, like Kekulé's on top of a London omnibus, in which a snake biting its own tail led him to the chemical structure of the benzene ring. Charles Darwin, beginning with his five-year voyage round the world in H.M.S. *Beagle*, patiently collected the observations for his theory of evolution. The key idea for his 'survival of the fittest' however, came from a book by an Anglican clergyman, Thomas Malthus, who suggested that populations always grow faster than the food and money for their support, leading to a struggle for survival.

Sir Karl Popper[4] considers that induction, drawing theories from facts, has little to do with science. His view is that scientists begin with a problem, produce a theory to explain it and then try to falsify the theory by doing more tests. Scientific theories then, are an approach to the truth, but never the final truth. Incidentally, for Popper the theory of evolution is metaphysics, not science, because it cannot be falsified. ('Just hang on for a million years, while I nip into the biology lab. and try it out'). Moreover, as Popper points out, evolutionary theory can explain almost too much. If space travellers found only six species of living creatures on a new planet, Darwinism would say that the conditions were suitable for only six. If the voyagers found just one, the answer would be that conditions were suitable for only one. More rigorous scientific theories can predict what will happen. Not so for evolution, which says that the various forms of life have survived because they are well adapted, or fit to survive: (what the schoolboy accidentally called 'the survival of the fattest'!). This amounts to saying that they survive because they survive.

When all is said and done, the secret of life still evades us. Living things are more complicated chemically than anything else we know of in the universe and so it is not surprising that we are less precise in our descriptions of them than in descriptions of say, rocks or sand. In many ways science now seems more modest than it was in Victorian times. In that confident era, physicists claimed that in principle they would soon know all that was to be known about the material world. Maxwell's electromagnetic theory brought together the understanding of electricity, magnetism and light. Matter was composed of indivisible atoms like minute billiard balls and its behaviour, even its future, was all predictable in terms of their positions and movements. Science would be the religion of tomorrow. Against it, all other human knowledge would be tried and found wanting.

Revolution in physics

That was the state of affairs in 1890. At the turn of the century an extraordinary change took place in physics, the fundamental experimental science. It was caused by the advent of quantum theory and relativity. In Stephen Leacock's words, 'It was Einstein who made the real trouble. He announced in 1905 that there was no such thing as absolute rest. After that there never was'. In the new physics, the atom is no longer a billiard ball, but a miniature solar system with a central positively-charged nucleus surrounded by spinning electrons. It seems to be largely empty space. And there are other odd features. Some experiments show that the electron is a tiny negatively-charged particle, others, equally reliable, that it is energy in the form of waves. Niels Bohr is supposed to have said that he believed in particles on Mondays, Wednesdays and Fridays, but waves on Tuesdays, Thursdays and Saturdays. The electron's behaviour can be expressed in the mathematical equations of wave mechanics but we can no longer picture it. Light also has this dual nature, behaving in some experiments as waves and in others as a stream of photons, discrete packets of energy. Until 1905 scientists were agreed that light consisted of waves of electromagnetic radiation. There was no other way to explain the pattern of light and dark stripes produced when light from two slits is allowed to fall on a screen. The reinforcements and cancellations are just what would be expected from waves. You can see the same thing when two sets of ripples from stones dropped in a pond interact with each other.

Another experiment, however, could only be explained if light was a stream of particles. When it shines on certain metals like selenium, electrons are ejected and the metal becomes electrically charged. This is the basis of the photoelectric cells used in burglar alarms. Only some of the electrons of the metal are shot out by the light – the ones which get a direct hit from a photon. By 1923, Compton had actually made such collisions visible, taking us back to the idea of light energy coming in small packets – something Sir Isaac Newton had believed long before.

So is light waves or particles? Both, it seems, but it is impossible to imagine it as a combination. Physicists have given up trying to picture it, as long as they can find mathematical ways of describing light. Dirac's quantum field theory paved the way in 1928 and Polkinghorne's book[5] gives a better account of all this and of the ultimate particles that make up matter than is possible here. He's a real physicist too!

Perhaps we can say that physicists have become introspective. They no longer claim confidently to describe the ultimate realities, but only to correlate their own experiences of nature. They are quite unlike the cosmologists who were described as 'often in error but never in doubt'.[6] The answers physicists get seem to depend on the experiments they do. The observer is all-important.

This is true in another sense. When we study individual atoms or smaller particles our experiments disturb them too much for us to see them as they really are. It is rather like taking a flash photograph of some shy nocturnal animal. You don't see him as he was before the flashlight disturbed him. Or suppose, to take a more precise example, that our eyes were sensitive to very short wave radiation and that we could illuminate an electron with this under a special microscope. To get more than just a blur, the wavelength of this 'light' would have to be very short indeed. However, the shorter the wavelength, the greater the energy. When the really short rays hit the electron they would knock it aside, so that although in theory we might see it, in practice the electron would not be there! We should have to return to longer-wave radiation and say that the electron was somewhere within the blur. This is a rough statement of Heisenberg's

18

famous 'Uncertainty Principle', which says that we cannot know both where a particle is and what it is doing. There is a limit to the accuracy with which position and momentum can be measured, because measuring the one will alter the other in a way we cannot completely control. For large objects like (real) billiard balls, this doesn't matter. The errors are so small as to be negligible. But for sub-atomic particles, comparable to the photons of light, the errors matter a lot. What is more, this is an absolute and final difficulty. It provides a full-stop the confident Victorians never dreamed of.

Yet more complexity

The sub-atomic world has become more complex since Einstein's day. Physicists now talk of anti-matter. The positron, for instance, is the opposite of an electron in every respect. If the two collided they would annihilate one another, leaving just a puff of energy, according to Einstein's well-known $E = mc^2$ equation; E being energy, m being mass and c the velocity of light. When I was a student there were two fundamental particles in the atomic nucleus, protons and neutrons, or so we were told. Now these each seem to consist of three quarks. Quarks come in four varieties, one known delightfully as a charmed quark. It may be that these four and the four members of the electron family (electron, heavy electron and two sorts of neutrinos) are the basic consitutents of matter. And it may not. A mere biochemist should not offer an opinion.

Indivisible billiard balls, then protons, neutrons and electrons, then a whole new family of particles with anti-matter to match: the message of atomic physics confirms Popper's view of science – theories waiting to be refuted rather than some fixed and final truth. Space physicist Professor Robert Boyd says much the same, that scientists 'know they do not really understand but merely picture to themselves the behaviour of God's world by insubstantial images of an ever elusive reality'.[7] It's rather like the Cheshire cat in Alice in Wonderland. Reality seems to have faded away, leaving just a grin. . . . or is it a frown?

In the attempt to understand, science seems to have taken everything to pieces, giving us a cold, dehumanized world of mechanisms. This 'reductionist' approach is essential to science. We explain inheritance in terms of genes and the behaviour of genes by studying the DNA molecules they contain. Yet the whole is usually more than the parts. Love is not merely an effect of certain steroid hormones, and your hopes and fears are not adequately described as patterns of electrical impulses among the nerve cells of your brain. My ginger cat (not Cheshire), sitting on the window sill as I write, may possibly be the result of chance mutations in a million million ancestors, but that hardly explains the elegance of his design, down to the last whisker.

Science describes how things work but it cannot tell us why things are as they are. Technology can neither produce a Rembrandt nor explain the ones we already have. Complete as it might be, who wants a scientific description of a Mozart symphony in terms of frequency patterns? If science provides the only road to truth, we may as well jettison most of the world's literature, art, music, philosophy and poetry. The mistake is easily made, since the scientific method can be applied to anything. Yet the great issues of life and death lie well beyond science. Attempts, for instance, to base moral codes on the natural sciences are doomed to failure. Evolutionary theory has been tried, the good being what survives, but this is merely the worship of success.

The Bible gives us a real basis for our morality. It is a book about right and wrong, about why we are here and why man, occasionally noble, has on the whole made such a mess of things. Above all, it is a book about the Creator of this extravagant and complicated universe, whose Son laid down his life for us. But that is another chapter.

3

Word of God?

3

Perhaps you find it hard to believe in a Creator. Oddly, the Bible does not seek to prove his existence by clever arguments. It does claim though that God has spoken, particularly through the prophets and history of his chosen people, the Jews. Wishful thinking on their part, you say, and how unfair to choose one small nation and ignore the rest of humanity!

The problems are real enough. But has God spoken? Can we really describe the Bible as his inspired word?

Forget your doubts for the moment and suppose that this universe is indeed the work of a benevolent Creator. Science can't prove that, but it can't disprove it either. Plenty of scientists, including some of the greatest, such as Newton and Einstein, could see the Designer's hand in what they studied. Suppose also that on a small planet in this universe is a creature the Designer is particularly pleased with, because so much of himself has gone into its making. Alone among living things this one can argue with God, and sadly, that is just what happens. Made free to love his maker, man turns away and his world becomes a dark place.

The Bible inspired?

The benevolent Creator is also the God of justice who hates evil. It would be possible to destroy the human race and start again, but instead he plans to restore the broken relationship. He tells one particular people about his love and justice but most of them reject the message so in the fullness of time he visits them himself. To be precise the Bible speaks of his sending his Son, Jesus Christ, but it also claims that 'God was in Christ' (2 Corinthians 5:19, Authorized Version). So, in a deep mystery it can be said that he died at their hands and his death provides forgiveness and restoration for all who turn to him from that time forward. So that all men can understand, the events are recorded, with suitable commentary, in a book. Needless to say, it becomes a best-seller.

If this was the way of it, the Bible must be the word of God. But why is it so difficult for twentieth-century man to accept? Perhaps because it sounds like a story from the Middle Ages, when the earth seemed the centre of the universe, enclosed by spheres which carried the planets and the sun. We have rejected that model for a very different one, a universe of vast, cold, empty spaces with countless suns and the earth merely an insignificant planet orbiting one of them. It is hard to believe that God could interest himself in such a speck. Or is it?

The argument from size is not convincing. Quite a modest amount of uranium–235 can destroy a city, and plague bacteria are too small to see, yet they can wipe out a whole population. Size tells us nothing about importance. Then there is life. The universe may have a myriad earths but life will be rare, intelligent life perhaps unique. Finally, fashions in models change. Who is to say that the present one will be the same in twenty years? Much of our resistance to the biblical account comes not from our own reasoning but from today's climate of thought. We are all conditioned by the age in which we live. Visitors to this planet become quite believable if they travel in spacecraft with all the trappings of modern technology. My favourite fictional visitor from outer space is ET. The film in which he starred seemed designed to rehabilitate Christianity, since ET came from the skies, could heal people and was eventually raised from the dead. Perhaps his popularity has something to do with our need to believe that we are not alone in a meaningless and unfriendly universe.

There is one other aspect of the size argument. The Creator of the galaxies cannot be less awesome than the universe he has made. Unless he has spoken, how can we expect to know him? Unless he makes himself small, how can we grasp him? As small in fact, as the baby who was called Immanuel, 'God with us'.

To say the least then, it is not unreasonable that the Bible was inspired by God. Sir Isaac Newton thought so. The great mathematician and physicist wrote a book on the prophecies of Daniel and the Revelation. For Newton, prophecy was not to satisfy our curiosity about the future, but to confirm our faith in the Bible. Scofield takes the same view and I have quoted him in the references[8].

The creation account

The biblical creation account is impressive too. Those first few chapters of Genesis are sublime in their simplicity and depth in comparison with the myths of Babylon, Egypt and ancient Greece. Some Christians, particularly in America, regard these chapters as scientific accounts in the modern sense, though they do not read like that and Kidner's excellent commentary[9] does not equate them with science. In fact they could not possibly be couched in modern scientific terms since the world-view of the modern scientist was unknown when they were written. A scientific description would hardly include a 'tree of the knowledge of good and evil'. No, the Bible is not a text-book of science: it has more important things to tell us about the nature of man[10], his broken relationship with his Creator and God's way of putting this right.

Nigel Cameron, in a recent well-argued discussion of evolution and biblical authority,[11] equates Darwinism with atheism, yet he admits that the Bible is not intended to be read as a scientific text-book. Nevertheless, Cameron adopts a 'creationist' interpretation of Genesis in which God makes a perfect world, possibly in six literal days, all suffering and death are the direct result of Adam and Eve's disobedience and later there is a universal flood. He is also sympathetic to Whitcomb and Morris's theory[12] that this flood produced all the fossils. Whether such an interpretation is really true to the Bible will be considered in later chapters, but one of the arguments for it needs to be considered now.

This argument concerns the authority and inspiration of the Bible and runs somewhat as follows. Old and New Testaments form one united book and do not contradict one another. In the New Testament Paul, and Jesus himself, quote passages from the Genesis creation account, thus giving a literalist interpretation the stamp of approval.

Now Jesus certainly accepted the Genesis account as authoritative, for instance when he referred to God's making male and female humans in discussing divorce.[13] But to argue that taking it as authoritative means that he was endorsing a particular literalistic interpretation is to beg the question. The argument assumes that the early chapters of Genesis were written as a plain factual narrative. Many reverent students of the Old Testament will disagree. Henri Blocher, for instance, in his book *In the Beginning*,[14] concludes that these chapters 'make theological statements about historical events which are described in a non-literal form.'

The other main argument[11] for accepting the Genesis account literally rests on Paul's comparison of Adam with Jesus in his letters to the Romans and Corinthians.[15] Adam is clearly taken as a historical figure whose disobedience brought sin and death into the world. Paul sets him against Jesus who brought us goodness and life. However, Paul's argument would be just as valid if other humans existed at the time of Adam. We cannot ignore Genesis 4:14 and

26

4:17 which may indicate that there were many other humans outside Adam's family. Then there are the mysterious verses about the sons of God and the daughters of men in Genesis 6. Those who insist that the world and all living things were made in six literal days and that Adam and Eve were the only humans existing on day six are not being as true to the Bible as they claim, since they are ignoring these later passages in Genesis.

As Kidner points out, the Bible agrees with modern science that the human race is genetically one. Kidner does consider the possible existence of 'pre-Adamites', as he calls them, alongside 'Adamites'. He comments as follows: ' . . . God may have now conferred His image on Adam's collaterals, to bring them into the same realm of being. Adam's "federal" headship of humanity extended, if that was the case, outwards to his contemporaries as well as onwards to his offspring, and his disobedience disinherited both alike'.[16]

Judging the Bible

This is not the place for a discussion of biblical inspiration, nor am I qualified to deal with the subject. For those who wish to read more, John Stott gives a balanced account.[17] Two points relating to science must be made though. First, while we can believe the Bible to be infallible when interpreted correctly and taken as a whole, we cannot read its picture language as modern science. Isaiah talks of the circle of the earth (40:22) and the ends of the earth (41:5) and elsewhere in the Old Testament we read of the pillars of the earth and its foundations. It would be just pedantic to criticize someone today for being scientifically inaccurate when he talked of the rising sun or the far corners of the earth.

Secondly, a statement made for a particular situation at a particular time must not be assumed to apply universally. In the moral realm, the doctrine of total war given on a certain occasion in Deuteronomy 20:16 ('do not leave alive anything that breathes') shows God's hatred of religious practices which included child sacrifice, but is clearly superseded by the teaching of Jesus.

Long before psychology became a science, the biblical writers gave us a searching account of human nature. There are those who consider man no more than a naked ape, only happy in the satisfaction of his animal appetites. Others see him gradually approaching perfection, master of his own fate, and now that he is come of age, needing no God to save him. Genesis presents us with a creature made in the image of his Creator but fallen, capable of greatness but so often failing to live up to his ideals; sick from a self-inflicted wound in his deepest being which only the forgiveness of God can heal.

How much truer to history and to our own experience is this view than the other two. We think we have found our heaven in love or beauty or wealth, but the vision fades and we are left unsatisfied. Jesus knew the human heart only too well: 'What good is it for a man to gain the whole world, yet forfeit his soul?' (Mark 8:36).

When all is said, there is really no way of judging the Bible, since it claims to be unique. It is no use comparing books of man's philosophy or science: if these find 'faults' in the Bible, how can we be sure that *they* are not wrong? When the Judge of all the earth humbled himself to become a man, earthly rulers and judges found him worthy of death. Yet at those trials he was really judging them.

The same may may well apply to our judgment of the Bible. We need a character judgment which cannot be made by the external methods of science. Many facts have been checked as correct from other historical or archaeological records. For instance, Sir Leonard Woolley's excavations have shown that Ur, the home of Abraham's family, was a highly developed city. At Ezion-Geber King Solomon's extensive smelting and refining plant for copper and iron has been unearthed. Luke's historical details have been checked at many points. In Acts 18:12 he mentions Gallio as Roman proconsul of Achaia, for example, and this is confirmed and dated by an edict of the Emperor Claudius inscribed on limestone and discovered at Delphi in Greece. Studies of this sort,[18] which are being made all the time, are bound to increase our confidence in the narrative.

Other statements of course cannot be checked like this. Who is to say whether the Ten Commandments are right or wrong, for instance? Science cannot make such judgments. At some point assumptions have to be made. Christians assume that man unaided could not know God's point of view and that God intervened in history to reveal it. Max Planck, the great physicist, said that 'Ye must have faith' was written over the entrance to the temple of science, too.

The evidence of experience

George Fox, the founder of the Society of Friends, came to know God in his own experience, in a sense experimentally. The Bible needs the same approach, very much that of the scientist in fact. It can only really be tested by seeing whether its words ring true. Of course whether you choose to believe it or not will not alter its objective, independent, eternal truth, but if you do not test it out in your own experience you can never come to a conclusion about it. This is especially so about the Bible's central character. Could he be the Son of God? If the record about Jesus is true, the rest will soon fall into place.

It is a matter of heart and will, not just intellect. 'If anyone chooses to do God's will, he will find out whether my teaching comes from God or whether I speak on my own', said Jesus.[19] The Bible has to be obeyed in faith before we can be sure about it. To read it with only scientific observations in mind is to gain very little; the authors had greater things in view than the study of nature. Their book is a plan to save the shipwrecked human race, not a philosophical discourse. It is a book to be lived, not merely discussed. St Paul called it 'the sword of the Spirit' and you cannot use a sword from an armchair!

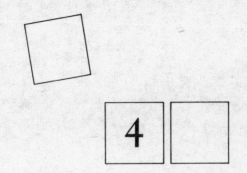

4

Chance and necessity

4

In 1970 Jacques Monod, molecular biologist and Nobel Prize-winner, published a startling book called *Chance and Necessity*. Its theme was that all life has developed as the result of random genetic mutations (see chapter 6) and therefore that man himself is an accident based on chance. From this, Monod argued that all traditional philosophy is worthless because it assumes a cosmic purpose and centres upon the human race. All the religions of the world and all its great thinkers from Plato to Hegel and Marx are wrong: 'The ancient covenant is in pieces; man at last knows that he is alone in the unfeeling immensity of the universe, out of which he emerged only by chance. Neither his destiny nor his duty have been written down'.

Having demolished most of human thought Monod sees his own bankruptcy. Who is to tell us what to do, how we should behave? The answer is a new 'ethic of knowledge' based on science and accepted in faith. Monod doesn't use the word faith, of course – man must 'impose it on himself' – but the meaning is the same. Monod misses a much greater problem, which leaves his argument in ruins. If all life is based on chance, man's mind must also be the result of purely irrational causes – not intelligent planning. If this is so, how can we expect our minds to be reliable and how can we take any argument seriously? C. S. Lewis[20] put it like this: 'Hence every theory which makes the human mind a result of irrational causes is inadmissible, for it would be a proof that there are no such things as proofs, which is nonsense'.

But does science really tell us that chance is at the heart of things? Einstein thought not: 'I shall never believe that God plays dice with the world'. 'Chance' can mean various things and we need to know what we are talking about when we use the word.

We sometimes confuse it with uncertainty. Heisenberg's Uncertainty Principle, mentioned in chapter 2, tells us about the limits of our knowledge in the sub-atomic world. We cannot specify the movements of an electron, but this does not mean that such movements are random. There is no reason to think that the electron does not obey laws of cause and effect, could we but see it.

If Monod was right, in what sense has life emerged 'by chance'? Certainly chance cannot *cause* anything, it is only a way of describing events. In this case 'by chance' seems to mean 'against all the odds' and most scientists would agree. From this Christians have reasoned that God must have created the first living things, the laws of science being inadequate to describe the origin of life. Others have said that the development of life was inevitable, given the condition of that primitive earth and the elements carbon, hydrogen, oxygen, nitrogen and so forth. Their word would be 'necessity', not chance. Neither view leads to the conclusion that life is an accident, that there is no master plan.

'There's a special providence in the fall of a sparrow', says Hamlet,[21] and the Bible certainly implies that for God there is no such thing as chance. Proverbs 16:33 could not be more specific: 'The lot is cast into the lap, but its every decision is from the LORD'.

There is something very much like casting lots at the

'*If we could just tap into the collective unconscious of the amoeba – then we'd know how it all began.*'

centre of the theory of evolution. Natural selection is thought to depend partly on small differences between individuals in a given population and these differences are due to mutations. More about them in chapter 6, but for the moment it is enough to say that they appear to be random events. If you grow bacteria in the laboratory, about one cell in ten million in each generation will be a mutant. It is impossible to predict which one, or what the mutation will be like. This is because mutations are essentially molecular events and something like Heisenberg's Uncertainty Principle operates. We cannot study individual molecules in sufficient detail to make predictions about them. If we knew enough, we should see that mutations obeyed laws of cause and effect, God's laws you might say. Monod is not logical then, in arguing from random mutations that there is no Creator. The whole process of evolution could be part of his eternal purpose.

The God of the gaps

While we are thinking about the theological as distinct from the scientific way of looking at things, two misguided approaches to nature need a few words. One of these is often called 'the God of the gaps'. When science seems to fail us we introduce God. Biochemists may know all about DNA and protein synthesis, we say, but no one has made life in the test tube. Therefore, only God can create life. Darwin, in *The Origin of Species* wrote of life having 'been originally breathed into a few forms or into one' – a passage echoing the description of God's creative activity in Genesis 2:7. After that special intervention the 'laws impressed on matter by the Creator' can take over, says Darwin, and there seems to be no further need of God.

Incidentally, this is not the biblical view of things. In both Old and New Testaments God is the creator and also the sustainer of the universe. Psalm 104:30 sums it up neatly when describing the natural world: 'When you send your

Spirit, they are created, and you renew the face of the earth'. St Paul quotes the Greek poet Epimenides[22] to make the same point: ' . . . he is not far from each one of us. For in him we live and move and have our being'. Another poet, Gerard Manley Hopkins, who was a Roman Catholic priest, puts it like this:

And for all this, nature is never spent;
  There lives the dearest freshness deep down things;
And though the last lights off the black West went
  Oh, morning, at the brown brink eastward, springs –
Because the Holy Ghost over the bent
  World broods with warm breast and with ah! bright
    wings.

This biblical view of nature as God's handiwork led to the development of experimental science in the Western Europe of the sixteenth and seventeenth centuries. In his book on this subject,[23] R. Hooykaas comments that 'whereas the bodily ingredients of science may have been Greek, its vitamins and hormones were biblical'.

To return to the God of the gaps, Newton provides a classic example. He could not explain the movements of the planets completely by his gravitational laws, so he asserted that God had to keep adjusting the solar system. In the next century Laplace's nebular hypothesis explained the system completely. In answer to Napoleon's question as to where God came in, he replied, 'Sir, I have no need of that hypothesis'. He was not advocating atheism, for he believed in God, but merely stating that God should not be brought in to fill a gap in our knowledge. The gap had been filled.

The God of the gaps mentality will always have that problem: the gaps get smaller. One day, even the origin of life may be understood in molecular terms. As mechanisms for this and that process are discovered, God appears to be left with less and less territory. But mechanisms are not everything. Science sets out to tell us how the universe works.

Knowing how does not make it happen. The laws of motion, as C. S. Lewis points out,[20] 'do not set billiard balls moving: they analyse the motion after something else ... has provided it'. The laws of science cover everything, though as yet incompletely, yet they leave out everything – 'the incessant torrent of actual events'. For the Christian, those are caused by God – or in the realm of human activities, since man is free, allowed by God.

Reductionism and complementarity

The other misguided approach to nature, in this case to living things, has been called 'reductionism'. Reductionists consider that the laws of physics and chemistry will ultimately explain everything in biology. For them, man is a complex machine whose operations are predictable from those laws.

Science mostly operates by breaking down complicated things into smaller units, but in biology the whole is usually more than the sum of the parts. To say that thought is merely a pattern of electrical impulses and love simply an effect of certain steroid hormones leaves us a long way from understanding Shakespeare as he wrote *Romeo and Juliet*. The statement that this page is a sheet of cellulose with small black marks on it is helpful as far as it goes, but the statement that it is part of a book on science and faith is more to the point. To say that is *merely* a cellulose sheet with black marks is misleading, not to say unkind!

This is not the prelude to a defence of 'vitalism', the old view that living matter has some non-physical organizing principle or vital essence. Nor do non-reductionists have to believe that man is a duality of body and soul, which is in any case a Greek, not a biblical view. No, the plea is that we should avoid what Donald MacKay calls 'nothing-buttery,[24] the idea that thought is 'nothing but electricity' or love 'nothing but hormones'. Living things need to be understood at various levels and descriptions at these different levels are complementary, even if they do seem to conflict. There is room for the view of man as a self-conscious personality responsible for his actions, even though it could all be completely represented in terms of neurons, electrical pulses, chemical transmitters and so on. The Bible itself provides alternative levels of description[25] and expects us to accept them both: we are made from dust, but made in the image of God.

This idea of 'complementarity' has appeared before when we were thinking of electrons. Are they waves or particles? We have to regard the two descriptions as complementary, even though they seem to contradict one another. The same applies to descriptions of living things, including the most difficult – the human brain. And finally, complementarity can embrace the scientific and religious descriptions of events. Paul for instance, tells us that at his conversion on the Damascus road he saw a vision from heaven and Jesus spoke to him. The same event could be described and to some extent understood in psychological terms – Paul's guilt at seeing Stephen killed and his own persecution of the Christians producing intolerable stress, and so forth. Yet the psychological approach should not deny the possiblity that Jesus spoke. The biblical description is complementary to the scientific one and science looks for 'cause and effect' explanations rather than 'purpose' explanations invoking God. Yet if it were not for that event on the Damascus road Europe might never have heard the Christian message and if Hooykaas[23] is right, science as we know it would never have developed.

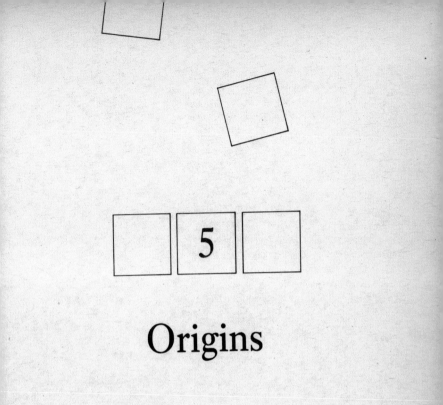

5

Origins

5

'The poor world is almost six thousand years old', says Rosalind in Shakespeare's *As You Like It*. When James Ussher, Archbishop of Armagh, wrote 'BC 4004' over the first verse of Genesis, the people of his time no doubt thought this a generous allowance for the age of the earth. Perhaps the more thoughtful raised an eyebrow when John Lightfoot calculated that Adam was created at 9 a.m. (forty-fifth meridian time) on October 23rd, 4004 BC. As a cautious scholar, the Chancellor of Cambridge University did not venture to commit himself any closer than this!

Today most geologists would put the age of the earth at 4,560 million years, give or take a year or two. Is the Bible wrong then, or had Ussher misunderstood the Genesis account? Some Christians today accept that account literally and believe that the universe was created in six days. They would consider that modifying their interpretation of Genesis in the light of modern science would undermine the authority of the Bible. Are they right? It all turns on what sort of scientific information, if any, those early chapters provide.

What are we to make of those genealogies for example? Even Whitcomb and Morris,[12] who accept the six-day creation and an earth of around ten thousand years old, admit that the lists are not strict chronologies. As Kidner[9] points out, the generations may not be in an unbroken chain.

Ten names are given from Adam to Noah, for instance (Genesis 5) and another ten from Noah to Abraham (Genesis 11). They may be selected as landmarks, rather than continuous links, just as happens in the stylized scheme of three fourteens in Matthew 1.

As to creation in six days, trying to understand Genesis 1–3 in this way gives us some real problems. Since the sun is not made until day four, how could the first three days have evening and morning in our sense? One explanation has been that heavy cloud hid the sun until day four, but the text does say '*made* two great lights' on that day (Genesis 1:16). It seems better not to press details and to follow the many scholars who understand 'day' to mean age or epoch. The word is certainly used like that elsewhere in the Bible. 'A thousand years in your sight are like a day' says Psalm 90:4, for instance, and Isaiah frequently uses 'day' to mean an indefinite future period when God will judge his people (*e.g.* 2:12, 3:18, 4:2).

The six days of creation

In Genesis 1 the order of creation is: ' in the beginning', heaven and earth; day one, light; day two, sea and sky; day three, dry land and plant life; day four, sun, moon and stars; day five, sea creatures and birds; day six, reptiles, animals and man. Genesis 2 goes over the same ground in more detail and is sometimes called a second creation account. It is really a commentary from the human point of view, logical rather than chronological, as Kidner puts it.[9] The narrative works outward from man and is localized in the 'garden in the east'. A sequence of events – Adam, garden of Eden, animals and birds, Eve – which would contradict Genesis 1 is probably not intended. It is interesting that the New International Version of the Bible, published in 1979, avoids this sequence by the wording, 'Now the LORD God *had* formed out of the ground all the beasts of the field and all the birds of the air' (Genesis 2:19) in the passage where they are brought to Adam to be named.

If we over-emphasize the literal we may miss deeper meanings. Augustine knew better: for him, the creation of Eve from Adam's rib taught the proper relation of man to woman. She was taken, he wrote, not from Adam's head to lord it over him, nor from his feet to be a servant, but from his side, near his heart, to be a companion. 'Bone of my bones and flesh of my flesh', says Adam. How much suffering could be avoided if our Western world had kept that high view of marriage.

The central facts of the early Genesis chapters are that God created everything and that man, made to know God and to be responsible for the world, turned away from his Creator. This disobedience involved more than the removal of fruit from a tree. Certainly Adam's *apple* does not appear in Genesis. However, whether or not the details are symbolic, there is no such thing as symbolic disobedience. The whole Genesis account of a world made good but spoilt by man sets the scene for the biblical history of redemption.

But why six days of creation? An omnipotent God could just as well have made the universe in one day, – or one second, presumably. Some scholars say that the account was written to justify the Jewish sabbath, a day of rest after six of work. That may be so, but for me the six days point to a more than human wisdom. They portray a majestic procession from earth through plant and animal life to man, not a scientific treatise but yet a remarkable foretaste of the account given by science today.

The Bible opens with the words, 'In the beginning God created the heavens and the earth'. Was there a beginning like this? About twenty years ago Fred (now Sir Fred) Hoyle put forward a theory of 'continuous creation' which seemed to do away with it. According to Hoyle the matter of the universe is being created all the time, from nothing, at an immeasurably slow, though calculable, rate. A uniform mean density is assured by the expansion of the universe, otherwise space would come to contain more and more matter. The universe is therefore infinitely old, though our own galaxy might only go back 5000 million years. Hoyle's theory was always controversial and is now rejected by most cosmologists. Instead, they accept the 'big bang' theory. This suggests that the universe began as an immensely dense ball of matter exploding to form the galaxies 10,000 million years ago, but does not tell us where the matter came from. Other estimates of the age of the universe range from 15,000 to 20,000 million years, cosmologists being pretty generous with their millions.

The 'big bang'

Of course, both theories contradict the law of conservation of mass-energy, which says that matter cannot be created. Einstein's famous equation $E = mc^2$ has already been mentioned in chapter 2. It indicates that matter is equivalent to an enormous amount of energy – the nuclear energy of the atom bomb, for instance. It certainly does not suggest that matter can be made out of nothing. So scientists cannot explain the origin of the universe and have to admit that it goes against one of their basic laws. Some indeed consider that this creation from nothing clearly implies the existence of a Creator.[26]

Evidence that the universe did have a definite beginning comes from several observations. One is the 'shift to the red' in the spectral lines from the light of distant galaxies, lines due to absorption by well-known chemical elements in the cooler gas within the galaxy. Their usual positions are known from the sun's spectrum. In the light from the distant stars they have a slightly longer wavelength than expected – they are moved towards the red end of the spectrum. This is the Doppler effect, discovered in 1842 by the Austrian physicist Christian Johann Doppler. Most of us have heard it when a fast train whistles as it passes. The pitch of the whistle goes up as the train approaches and falls as it recedes from us. More sound waves per second strike the eardrum when the train is approaching so the sound is higher. It is the same with light waves. The opposite happens when the source of light is going away from us; fewer waves per second arrive at the eye and the light looks redder, of lower frequency and longer wavelength. The 'red shift' then, shows that the stars are moving away from us. Wherever we look the same happens: the whole universe is expanding. But it cannot have been expanding for ever. At some point it began to expand, with that 'big bang'.

Another line of evidence depends on a mysterious abstraction called *entropy*. It is as if the machinery of the universe is gradually running down. Whenever one form of energy is converted into another, some energy is lost as heat: superheated steam driving turbines and dynamos to make electricity for instance, or the energy from your food being used to make muscles work so that you can run. This useless heat is called entropy and it is always being produced. The second law of thermodynamics says that entropy is increasing as time goes on. A physicist who was a bit of a wag put it like this: 1 You can't win, you can only break even. 2 You can only break even at absolute zero. 3 You can't ever reach absolute zero (−273°C).

Since heat is essentially random movements of molecules, another way of putting the second law is to say that things get more disorderly. 'Shuffling is the thing Nature never undoes', said Sir Arthur Eddington. The universe seems rather like a clock which is gradually running down. At some time in the past then, when entropy was zero, it must have been wound up. That winding up was the cosmic beginning.

These arguments rely on the concept that the laws of science are unchanging. Most people assume this and without the assumption it would hardly be worth slogging away in the laboratory. But how did it arise? Discussing the origins

47

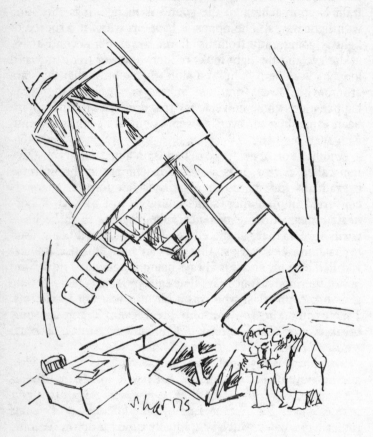

'*The only part of the universe which* isn't *expanding is the budget for this place.*'

of natural science, C. S. Lewis[20] says, 'Men became scientific because they expected Law in Nature, and they expected Law in Nature because they believed in a Legislator'. As already mentioned, Hooykaas expands the same thought.[23] For the atheist, uniformity is just an assumption, an article of faith. Even atheists have to believe in something!

The age of the earth

Estimates of the earth's age mostly depend on radioactive dating these days, though in the last century Lord Kelvin calculated from the rate of cooling of a once molten earth. Radioactive elements act as geological clocks since they 'decay' to a more stable element at a constant rate, emitting charged particles or gamma rays. Each radioactive element then has a particular and exact 'half-life', the time taken for half its atoms to decay. For instance, the uranium and thorium in rocks finally decay to lead. While the rock was still molten, the lead diffused away from its place of origin. Once the material solidified, lead accumulated alongside the uranium and thorium at a constant rate, so a measure of their relative amounts give the age of the rock. Such methods show that some rocks solidified only 3,000 million years ago. The oldest identified is a volcanic rock from West Greenland 3,824 million years old.

Rocks from the moon and meteorites thought to come from a belt between the orbits of Mars and Jupiter have been dated to 4,600 million years. Comparisons of lead isotope ratios in meteorites and various rocks on earth suggest that our planet is also about 4,600 million years old. This pleases the astronomers, who have other reasons for thinking that the whole solar system had a single origin.

Defenders of six-day creation[12] are of course very critical of radioactive dating, since they believe the earth to be only about ten thousand years old. However, errors in the method are not likely to produce ages a million times too great and this is admitted by the creationists. Instead, they resort to the 'apparent age' theory first propounded in Darwin's day. This says that God created the rocks with just such ratios of elements within them as would have been produced by radioactive decay over millions of years. We shall meet this idea again in chapter 8.

Scientists agree then that the universe had a beginning, making belief in a Creator not unreasonable, to say the very least. But science will not lead us to him. It is easy to get lost in the by-ways of natural theology and to overlook the direct route: 'I am the way', said Jesus,[27] ' . . . No-one comes to the Father except through me'.

6

Primaeval soup

6

Writing in the 1929 *Rationalist Annual*, J. B. S. Haldane envisaged the origin of life in a primitive ocean which had become a 'hot dilute soup' as light from the sun produced organic molecules from carbon dioxide and ammonia in the atmosphere. He made the process seem quite easy and natural. Half a century later we know much more about living cells. The astronomer Sir Fred Hoyle recently commented that the idea of life arising by random shuffling of constituent molecules was 'as ridiculous and improbable as the proposition that a tornado blowing through a junk yard may assemble a Boeing 747'. Incidentally, to judge from his earlier book on cosmology,[28] which ridiculed belief in God, Hoyle does not write from a Christian standpoint.

Not so very long ago people believed in the spontaneous generation of life. In 1837 Andrew Cross claimed that a small bettle could be produced by electrolysis of suitable solutions. He even named it as a new species – *Acarus galvanicus!* Spontaneous generation goes back to Aristotle, though Augustine quaintly observed that if it really could happen there would have been no need for Noah's ark. The great Louis Pasteur finally laid spontaneous generation to rest in the mid-nineteenth century, with his studies of fermentation by micro-organisms in the air. He met considerable opposition, often on rationalist grounds. Haeckel, for instance, claimed that spontaneous generation must be true, not because it could be confirmed in the laboratory, but because otherwise it would be necessary to believe in a Creator.

The best-known experiment on the origin of the 'building blocks of life', or some of them, is that of Stanley Miller in 1953. He passed electric discharges through a mixture of methane, ammonia, hydrogen and water vapour, forming traces of amino acids and other small molecules found in living organisms. The discharges could clearly represent electric storms on a primitive earth, but scientists are now doubtful about that particular mixture of gases. It seems more likely that the young earth had an atmosphere of carbon dioxide and water vapour with smaller amounts of nitrogen and carbon monoxide. Geologists agree that there was no oxygen, which means that there was a great deal of ultraviolet radiation from the sun. Most of this is now kept out by ozone formed from oxygen in the upper atmosphere. Ammonia was essential for the development of life, yet ultraviolet rays rapidly convert it to nitrogen. It was difficult to see how there could ever have been enough ammonia until the recent suggestion that the catalytic action of titanium dioxide in desert sands produced it from nitrogen.

Carbon dioxide could have been a problem too. More than a certain amount in the atmosphere would have produced an inferno by the 'greenhouse effect'. Too little and there would have been a permanent ice-age like that of Mars. If our earth is not unique, it is a very rare place. The origin of life was probably a close-run thing, from our point of view!

The origin of life

When did life begin? Using the American billion (1000 million) the earth is thought to be 4.56 billion years old and geologists find microfossils of single-cell organisms in rocks which may date back 3.5 billion years. Those first living things had to feed on the 'primaeval soup' and oxygen would have killed them. Life seems to have stayed in that single cell form for more than 2 billion years if we are to believe the record of the rocks. Only in the Cambrian period (0.6 billion years ago) does the fossil record show a remarkable burst of activity in the formation of complex creatures. Why the long delay? Food was probably the major problem. The soup would soon have become too thin to support life unless photosynthesis had developed. Bacteria and blue-green algae gained the ability to make foodstuffs from the carbon dioxide of the air by this means, and in turn to produce oxygen. This eventually revolutionized the whole scheme of things by providing much more food. In addition the oxygen protected life from the sun's ultraviolet rays. But it was a pretty slow revolution. Incidentally there is still argument about the source of today's oxygen. Some may have come from the action of light on water and not from photosynthesis.

So much for the scenario as scientists now envisage it, but we passed rather glibly over the origin of life. Assuming that reactions like Miller's could produce the simple molecules of the soup, we are still a long way from the first living cell. The key thing about such cells is that they contain very large molecules, the essential ones being proteins and the nucleic acids DNA and RNA. Their molecular weights are in the hundred thousand to million range while Miller's products have weights of only about 200. Proteins, for instance, are like chains of hundreds of beads. There are about twenty different sorts of beads (amino acids) and they are put together in a very special order. To work properly, each protein must have exactly the right sequence of beads and the possibilities are endless. For a 'hundred-bead' protein there are 20^{100} different sequences – roughly 10 with 129 noughts after it! Fig. 1 shows a protein of about this size – pro-insulin, the precursor of the hormone diabetics lack. There are 81 amino acid 'beads', the abbreviated name being written on most of them. Dr Fred Sanger of Cambridge was awarded

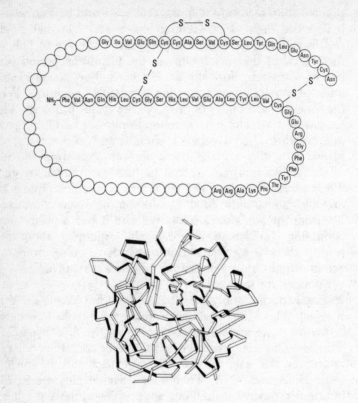

Fig. 1 *The top picture is of pro-insulin. Amino-acid 'beads' without a label are removed in the final processing to make insulin. The bottom picture shows how an imaginary globular protein might fold itself.*

a Nobel Prize in 1958 for establishing the sequence of the amino acids in insulin and another one in 1980 for the even more difficult task of 'sequencing' DNA. The figure also shows a model of a protein with its chain folded up in a complicated way. This can be deduced by a special X-ray technique and there is only one correct way of folding any particular protein. Unless it is folded correctly it doesn't work and its specific sequence of amino acids makes it fold in that special way under normal conditions.

The genes which determine our make-up, passing on characteristics from our parents, are found in the chromosomes of the nucleus of each cell in our bodies. Genes are made of DNA, another long-chain molecule with four sorts of beads called nucleotides. The arrangement of these nucleotides can be copied into another long molecule, messenger RNA, and then used by the protein-making machinery of the cell (Figs. 2 and 3) to produce the exact sequence of amino acid beads in each protein.

We say that DNA contains the 'genetic code', a message written in a four-letter alphabet along the DNA chain. It seems that everything the cell needs to know is written there. If we are right about that, the problem of the origin of life comes down to the problem of arranging a DNA or perhaps RNA necklace of say 10,000 beads in the correct order. In such a case there would be $10^{8,000}$ possible arrangements, a vast number! Then you must stick the nucleotide beads together – a process needing a great deal of chemical energy.

Manfred Eigen, physical chemist and another Nobel Prize-winner, suggests that a smaller (80 bead) RNA molecule appeared first. We know that the four nucleotide beads of DNA or RNA can stick together in pairs and Eigen believes that the sequence of beads which could best protect itself by looping up so that its beads stuck together was the first sequence to form. However, this trial and error mechanism would not produce molecules bigger than about 25,000 molecular weight, while the RNA of living cells is hundreds of times bigger. Eigen and Schuster have ideas for bridging the gap by what they call 'hypercycles', but the problems are formidable and scientists have not been very keen to accept these ideas.

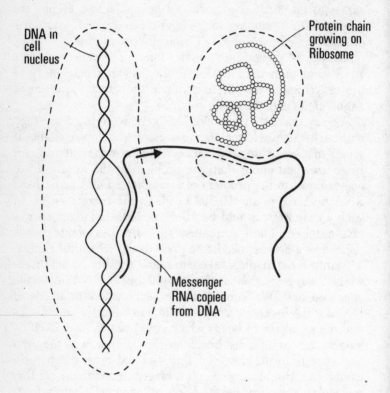

DNA in
cell
nucleus

Protein chain
growing on
Ribosome

Messenger
RNA copied
from DNA

Fig. 2 *A simplified diagram of how cells make protein.*

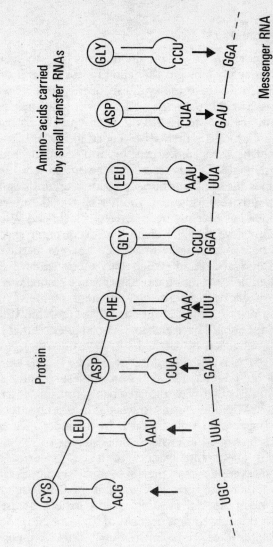

Fig. 3 *A more detailed look at the protein factory at the point where amino-acids are linked on the ribosome to make a protein.*

God's special work?

Sir Karl Popper puts the difficulty like this ' . . . the genetic code is without any biological function unless it is translated; that is unless it leads to the synthesis of the proteins whose structure is laid down by the code. But . . . the machinery by which the cell . . . translates the code consists of at least fifty proteins which are themselves coded in DNA. Thus the code cannot be translated except by using certain products of its translation'.[29] The chicken and the egg in fact.

Sometimes the apparent miracle of life's origin is 'solved' by conveniently removing it to another part of the universe. This old idea has recently been revived. Hoyle and Wickramasinghe[30] believe that life came here from outer space in the form of a micro-organism. They are not particularly impressed by Darwin and evolutionary theory either, seeing great difficulties in the idea that chance mutations are sufficient to account for the development of life. Francis Crick, who once rebelled at the idea that Churchill College in Cambridge should have a chapel, also suggests[31] that some mystical Intelligence dispatched life to the earth from the depths of space. Crick shared a Nobel Prize for his work on DNA, so he understands the problems surrounding the origin of life. His theory of 'directed panspermia' is described as follows: 'Microorganisms travelled in the head of an unmanned spaceship sent to earth by a higher civilization which had developed elsewhere some billions of years ago'. Tall stories about Intelligences in distant galaxies solve nothing however. Perhaps they show that science is at the end of its tether when trying to account for life's beginning.

At this point 'special creation' seems to leap at us. But what about the subsequent pageant of life – orchids, orangoutangs, butterflies, boa-constrictors, ducks, dinosaurs, hedgehogs and humans? Is this not special too? The whole creative process is God's special work. As Sir Thomas Browne put it:[32] 'All things began in order, so shall they end, and so shall they begin again; according to the ordainer of order and mystical mathematics of the city of heaven'.

Talking of order reminds me of a criticism some Christians have of evolutionary ideas. The origin and development of life, they say, is a process of increasing order and complexity. Yet as we have seen in the previous chapter, the second law of thermodynamics says that as time goes on, things get less orderly, so evolution cannot be true. The argument sounds plausible until you remember that the earth is not an isolated planet. We depend on the sun's energy. Living things can use this energy to combat entropy as it were. Yet taking the whole solar system, the loss of order as the sun burns itself out is greater than the gain shown by the living world. Of course, if the physicists are correct, the sun has a limited life and one day the earth will become too cold to support life of any sort.

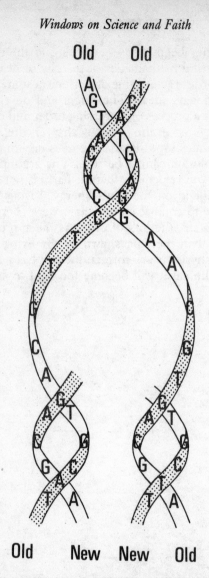

Fig. 4 *How DNA is replicated when a cell divides. The two parent strands (marked 'old') separate and each is copied. The daughter cells will have DNA with one old strand and one new.*

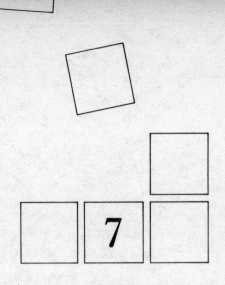

7

Molecules and mutations

7

Evolutionary theory seeks to explain the origin of species by small differences between individuals in a population having 'survival value'. The differences are due to mutations and these can be understood if we take another look at DNA. This large molecule which controls the synthesis of protein (and probably the whole behaviour of the cell) is a sequence of thousands of nucleotide beads with four to choose from, A, T, G and C for short. The exact sequence is inherited from the parents of the organism and provides the chemical basis of genetics. Genes are essentially DNA and the nucleotide sequence makes a message in a four-letter alphabet. Part of the 'message' might read GTTGAGGCTTGC, for example. When a cell divides, its DNA, which is a double strand of beads, has to be replicated so that each daughter cell has the original amount.

As the diagram on p. 62 shows, the copying depends on the 'stickiness' of the beads – A sticks to T and G to C. The copying process is very accurate but occasionally there is a mistake and the wrong bead goes in or one is left out altogether. If this happens in the germ cells of an animal for instance, the next generation will have a new DNA which codes for a slightly different (or very different) protein – a mutation has taken place. Most mutations will be harmful, even killing the embryo, but a very few will be beneficial. Apart from copying errors, radiation or poisonous chemicals can cause mutations.

The DNA code

The entire chemical composition of any living creature is controlled by its proteins, since many proteins are enzymes, catalyzing and controlling the production of various substances. As outlined in the previous chapter, each protein 'necklace' has a special sequence of amino-acid 'beads' and this sequence gives the protein its special character. Unless it is more or less correct, the protein will not work properly in the chemical factory of the cell. As you can see from figs. 2 and 3 (pp. 58–59), three of the nucleotide beads in messenger RNA, which is a copy of nuclear DNA, tell the protein-making machinery which amino-acid bead to put into the growing protein necklace. Those three nucleotide beads, for instance UCA, which codes for the amino-acid serine, are called a codon. We talk about the genetic code. All living things seem to use this same genetic code, just as they have many identical chemical components. This suggests that they are closely related and that all forms of life had a common origin.

The effects of mutations can be seen by comparing the amino-acid 'bead' sequence in samples of a particular protein such as cytochrome c, from different living organisms. Cytochrome c is part of the power house of the cell where food is converted to energy, so it is an important protein. Its exact shape, which has to fit an iron-containing haem molecule inside the protein, depends on the amino-acid sequence as we have seen already. Changing some of the beads alters the shape so much that the cytochrome c cannot function – the cell would lose power, and such mutations would be lethal.

But changing other beads makes little difference.

Over the generations, these changes which have relatively little effect become fixed in the cytochrome c and so, if you compare this protein from a mouse, a man or a frog, for instance, you will see small differences. Cytochrome c from many different living things has therefore been 'sequenced' and the sequences compared. There are 104 amino-acid beads in its necklace and for man and the chimpanzee the sequence is identical. Comparing the human sequence with a single cell bread mould, on the other hand, we find 44 differences. Other proteins, for example haemoglobin, the red pigment of blood, can be used in the same way to see how closely related the higher animals are. The differences provide a numerical measure of the degree of relatedness between species. They are free from human bias and can be used to draw one of those evolutionary family trees by computer. It turns out to be much the same as that derived from the fossil record. In fact, if the fossils had never been discovered, this molecular study would push us to much the same conclusions as those of Darwin and the more traditional biologists.

Those who believe that God created each species separately would reject this line of argument. They would say that each species has its own special cytochrome c with an amino-acid sequence which exactly fits its own needs. This is probably true, but what has been called the molecular clock is hard to explain from a creationist standpoint.

The origin of species?

What is this molecular clock? Biochemists have compared the human cytochrome c sequence with that of the other organisms and then looked at the length of time the various species are thought to have been in existence, using the fossil record and the ages of the rocks determined by radioactive dating. The older the species, the more its sequence differs from the human protein. What is more, plotting the supposed age of the species against the number of differences gives a straight line. The same applies to a number of proteins which have been studied in this way. In other words, there is a steady rate of change in the sequences, one amino acid change being fixed in about a million years for cytochrome c. The rate of change is different for other proteins, but for all of them, a sort of biological clock ticks slowly away.

If all living species were created in six days, or over a relatively short span of time, as some creationists say, it is difficult to see why the sequences should show this steady rate of change when fitted to the fossil record. A constant mutation rate over a long time period provides a reasonable explanation.

Yet we are still a long, long way from the origin of species. In fact we know precious little in molecular terms of how evolution might work. Mutations may be at the heart of it, but most of the differences between a frog and an elephant say, are not understood in terms of the genetic code. We know how DNA controls the making of proteins like cytochrome c, but these are much the same in all living creatures. We need to know how growth and development are controlled, why legs or brains or noses are a particular shape. How did the single fertilized egg from which each of us grew manage to produce all the different types of cells which go to make up skin and nerves, muscles and bones? Until we know more about the marvels of embryology we are not likely to understand the origin of species.

One clue may come from what is called 'silent DNA'. All organisms have far more DNA than is needed to code for their proteins. Perhaps the extra DNA controls growth and development. However it works, the control is remarkable. Worn skin, for instance, is replaced so carefully that fingerprints can identify us. The more we learn of living things, the more impressed we are by the marvellous intricacy of their design. Though mutations look like accidents, it would be going far beyond the scientific evidence to say that the development of life on this planet followed no plan. Pondering embryology long before it was a science, the psalmist[33] saw further than DNA:

> For you created my inmost being;
>   you knit me together in my mother's womb.
> I praise you because I am fearfully and wonderfully
>   made; . . .
> When I was woven together in the depths of the earth,
>   your eyes saw my unformed body.
> All the days ordained for me
>   were written in your book
>   before one of them came to be.

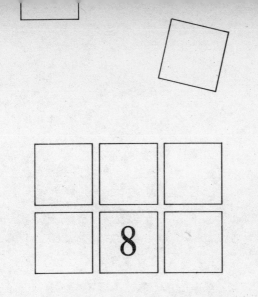

Evolution

8

Darwin's theory of evolution upset many of the Christians of his day and still generates controversy more than a century later. Some of the trouble goes back to the famous 1860 meeting of the British Association in Oxford, when Bishop Samuel Wilberforce attacked Darwin's ideas, finishing with a flourish by asking Thomas Huxley whether he was related to a monkey through his grandfather's or his grandmother's side of the family. Huxley ('Darwin's bulldog') produced an equally lively response, commenting that he would rather be related to an ape than to an obscurantist bishop. Darwin was not there, but wrote to Huxley in nervous delight when he heard the news: ' . . . how durst you attack a live bishop in that fashion? I am quite ashamed of you! Have you no respect for fine lawn sleeves? By jove, you seem to have done it well!'

Huxley, who coined the word *agnostic*, was a self-made man, born in humble accommodation over a butcher's shop in Ealing. He left school at 10, but by 26 his biological researches had gained him a Fellowship of the Royal Society. Nevertheless the dreaming spires of Oxford were symbols of privileges he had never enjoyed and a patronage he despised. Oxford and Cambridge were entirely under ecclesiastical control and most important teaching posts went to clergymen. At the British Association in 1860 the Bishop of Oxford represented far more than an attempt to demolish Darwin's theory. To Huxley and many others he represented control of university education by an ecclesiastical establishment and the suppression of truth by priests. So the debate about evolution and the Bible was inflamed and distorted by a struggle against power politics in education which was a separate issue altogether.

Darwin's theory says that favourable variations in animals or plants tend to survive and that over many generations such small variations lead to new species. Though we know something of how changes in DNA could cause these variations we do not understand how a new organism could develop, or even a new organ, like an eye. With the addition of the protein sequence work outlined in chapter 7 and the experimental studies mentioned below, the evidence for evolution has much the same strengths and weaknesses as when Darwin first put it together.[34] Briefly it consists of the great age of the earth and the fossil record, comparative anatomy showing similar structures in widely different species, modification of plants and animals by domestic breeders, vestigial organs like the 'tail' of a human embryo and changes due to geographical distribution. Colin Patterson[35] has written a balanced and readable modern account.

The scientific theory under attack

Setting aside religious arguments, how does evolution stand today as a scientific theory? It is certainly accepted by most biologists, probably because if offers an explanation of the relationships between many living organisms and brings them into a system. There was a time when biology consisted largely of descriptions of thousands of species, more cataloguing than understanding. Physical scientists rudely referred to it as stamp collecting. Darwin's theory, and the more recent molecular genetics, take biology a little way towards hard rather than soft science and are naturally welcomed for that reason.

'I don't know either. Go back to the ship and get Mr Darwin.'

Nevertheless, there are critics of evolution as a theory. Popper's complaint that it explains too much and is metaphysics rather than science because it cannot be refuted, has been mentioned already in chapter 2 (p. 16). Most biologists would disagree with Popper, pointing out that evolutionary theory provides many specific hypotheses which could have been refuted by experiment, but have not been. For instance it predicts that when organisms are classified by different characteristics, the same branching 'family tree' of relationships will be found. There is also experimental evidence that natural selection can bring about evolutionary change quite rapidly – for example a laboratory change of 1% per generation in fruit fly morphology compared with 1% per million years in the fossil record of the horse.

Louis Bounoure, the French biologist, regards evolution as a myth, something which cannot be tested experimentally, arising not from nature but from man's mind and easily made a dogma.[36] The zoologist Pierre Grasse[37] finds natural selection and mutations inadequate to explain the development of new species. Though sympathetic to evolutionary theory, Kerkut[38] believes that the evidence supporting it is too weak for it to be considered more than a working hypothesis. Like most authors quoted here, he wrote before the molecular biology of chapter 7 provided new evidence.

One of the anti-Darwinian classics is *The Transformist Illusion* by Douglas Dewar[39] and though some of its criticisms are out-dated, the inadequacy of the fossil record is shown clearly. Incidentally, Darwin himself admitted as much: 'The case at present must remain inexplicable; and may be truly urged as a valid argument against the views here entertained'.[34]

The late Professor Ernst Chain of Imperial College London was also critical of evolution, which he called 'a hypothesis based on no evidence and irreconcilable with the facts'.[40] E. F. Schumacher[3] distinguished between biological evolution, the description of biological change from the fossil record, and Evolutionism, the doctrine that its cause, natural selection, was automatic, with no room for divine guidance or design. Evolutionism he called 'science fiction, even a kind of hoax'.

Some Christians have tried to dismiss the fossil record. Philip Henry Gosse, a fine biologist of Darwin's day, had no time for evolution – 'a scheme by which the immediate ancestor of Adam was a chimpanzee and his remote ancestor a maggot'. Gosse wrote a book called *Omphalos*,[41] meaning navel, the central theme being that God's creation of a mature world in six days would inevitably produce an appearance of age. Adam would have had a navel for instance, even though he was not born of a woman and the trees of the Garden of Eden would have had rings suggesting many a previous summer and winter. Likewise, though this is harder to follow, the rocks will have been created with fossils in them. Gosse admitted that 'to assume the world to have been created with fossil skeletons in its crust – skeletons of animals that never really existed – is to charge the Creator with forming objects whose sole purpose was to deceive us'. Which is just what the book reviewers said. Gosse's attempt to reconcile geology and a literal view of Genesis was ridiculed by most of them.

Some limitations to the theory

Perhaps because Darwin's theory was attacked by theologians and others from the very beginning, biologists have usually been rather defensive, if not over-protective, when discussing evolution. At present they seem more open. Several eminent biologists outline limitations of the theory in a recently published *Encyclopedia of Ignorance*.[42] Many other problems about Darwinism are detailed by the late Gordon Rattray Taylor,[43] who quotes von Bertalanfly as follows: 'I think the fact that a theory so vague, so insufficiently verifiable . . . has become a dogma can only be explained on sociological grounds'.

Evolution has usually been thought to proceed very gently in the production of new species, but there is now argument about this. Biologists such as Stephen Jay Gould suggest a 'punctuated equilibrium' model with sudden quite large-scale changes. This is partly because the fossil record contains so few 'missing links' between species and partly because the mutation rate is considered too slow to account for all the changes. Michael Ruse,[44] in a book called *Darwinism Defended* gives an account of the controversy. Part of it is concerned with classification. Cladism, a new method of classification, is based on branching in the tree of life and is happy with sudden changes. Some Christian writers have argued that cladism goes against evolutionary theory altogether and supports special creation. Gould would certainly not accept those views.

If there are so many criticisms of the theory of evolution, can we put a better theory in its place? Considering the scientific facts only, the answer is probably no, because we understand so little about the control of growth and form, as I have said already. It does seem that life began simply and that more complex organisms appeared over a long span of time, the sequence ending with man. The punctuated equilibrium theory recalls the view of some Christian writers that mutations and selection may account for minor development but that divine intervention produced the major changes. Alan Hayward[45] for instance, talks of many separate creative acts of God in the long history of the earth. This theory of successive creation cannot be proved or disproved since it takes us outside science. Scientists are now trying to find explanations at the molecular level and will not be satisfied by a theory which says God is continually manipulating the molecules in a series of small miracles.

No doubt evolutionary theory is inadequate in many ways, but we must remember the 'God of the gaps'. In a very balanced book on science and religion, Ian Barbour[46] quotes the physical chemist C. A. Coulson quite aptly: 'When we come to the scientifically unknown, our correct policy is not to rejoice because we have found God; it is to become better scientists'. Charles Kingsley, an Anglican clergyman and a friend of both Charles Darwin and Philip Gosse, could welcome evolution, which he saw as a 'chapter of special Providences of Him without whom not a sparrow falls to the ground'. 'The choice', he wrote, 'is between the absolute empire of accident and a living, immanent, ever-working God . . .'. When we consider ourselves, that choice becomes even more important, as the next chapter seeks to show.

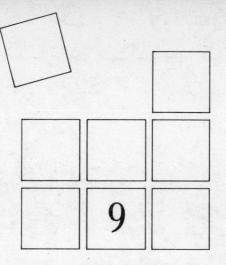

9

Man in God's image?

9

On reading Darwin's views that we were descended from the monkeys, the wife of an Anglican bishop is supposed to have said, 'Well, let us hope that it is not true, or if it is, that it will not become generally known'. Now the wheel has come full circle and it is popular these days to dwell on the animal side of man's nature, to describe him as merely a naked ape. No doubt we have much in common with the animals, but is naked ape a fair description?

The Bible states quite clearly that man was made in the image of God (Genesis 1:27) and its whole message conveys human dignity and responsibility. Can we keep our self-respect or must we consider ourselves glorified animals? Biologically speaking, there is an enormous difference between *homo sapiens* and the higher apes. There is no Darwinian explanation of human culture. Even Michael Ruse, who appears to have no particular respect for the Bible and is pretty hard on the American creationists, sees 'nothing yet that even scratches at an explanation of how a transformed ape could produce the magnificence of Beethoven's choral symphony'.[44] It seems quite reasonable to describe our appreciation of beauty and our understanding of right and wrong in terms of 'the image of God', remembering that we have marred that image pretty considerably. Bernard Shaw cynically remarked that our true genius now lies not in art or science, but in the design of the weapons of war.

Darwin's natural selection depends on species adapting themselves to specialized environments but the theory does not apply at all well to man, since humans are remarkably unspecialized. If we originated in African savannahs we can also manage quite well in the Arctic, in deserts or in tropical rain forests. The Darwinian answer (an example of evolutionary theory explaining everything, or nothing, and of evolutionists wanting to have it both ways) would be that man developed adaptability, perhaps by being exposed to more than one environment. But how, no-one knows. Darwinians would say that man is adapted to all sorts of environments by his lack of specialization.

Homo sapiens provides other problems for the theory of evolution. Why, for instance, do we have such large brains? On the face of it, bigger brains providing greater intelligence should have survival value. Yet S. J. Gould[47] is not too happy about the details: 'But why did such a large brain evolve in a group of small, primitive, tree-dwelling mammals, more similar to rats and shrews than to mammals conventionally judged as more advanced? . . . we simply do not know . . .'

In his *Descent of Man*, Darwin argued that we are descended from the apes, but he had to confess that man's moral nature could not be explained. Why should altruism have survival value? 'He who was ready to sacrifice his life, as many a savage has been, rather than betray his comrades, would often leave no offspring to inherit his noble nature', wrote Darwin. Biologists who puzzle over this today think in terms of small tribes rather than individuals and see altruism as enlightened self-interest. The unselfish person helps the group, they say, but in my view the puzzle remains unsolved.

It is not surprising then, that some biologists, the best-known being E. O. Wilson,[48] have explained human society and culture in terms of an evolved human nature. The implication is that our genes determine our social behaviour. Even animal 'sociobiology', as the subject is called, is highly speculative and since it is so difficult to assess environmental as distinct from genetic influences, some biologists consider that sociobiology cannot be applied at all to man. In his criticism of this controversial subject, Kenneth Bock[49] sees it 'reducing history to biological events and so losing touch with the very stuff of human life'.

The late David Lack,[50] an eminent biologist as well as a Christian, had doubts about the ability of science to explain the origin of man. He considered that biologists have not accounted for morality, truth, beauty or self-awareness and yet if man has evolved by wholly natural means, all human nature should be interpretable in scientific terms. 'It might therefore be argued', wrote Lack, 'that man cannot have evolved wholly by natural means'.

The early chapters of Genesis

It is now time to get to grips with the early chapters of Genesis. Are we to regard the Adam and Eve account as a myth, with no historical relevance at all, as some theologians say? At the other extreme, are we to insist that the human race began with a single pair about 6,000 years ago? Before tackling this most difficult topic let me make two points. First, I can only present a personal view and admit that the scientific facts about primitive man are not plentiful and that anthropologists change their views fairly regularly. Second, Genesis may give less support to the single pair view than the creationists admit. Even if we grant that Cain's wife was one of his sisters, we still have a group of people east of Eden from whom he had to be protected after murdering his brother. They could have been younger brothers, but the impression I get from Genesis 4:14–16 is that they were strangers and that the region was quite well populated. For a related discussion from two different viewpoints see Berry and Wright in '*Creation and Evolution*' (details on p. 125f.).

Linked with Adam and Eve is the question of what theo-

logians call original sin. Adam is clearly referred to in
Romans 5 as the *one* man through whom sin entered the
world, and through sin came death. (At a later point we shall
have to consider whether death means physical death in this
context.) Pope Pius XII in his 1950 encyclical *Humani generis*,
roundly warned the faithful that 'Christians cannot lend their
support to a theory which involves the existence, after
Adams's time, of some earthly race of men, truly so called,
who were not descended ultimately from him, or else
supposes that Adam was the name given to some group of
our primordial ancestors'. 'It does not appear', the encyclical
goes on, 'how such views can be reconciled with the doctrine
of original sin . . . committed in actual historical fact, by an
individual named Adam . . .'

Anthropologists consider that creatures physically similar
to modern man existed at least 100,000 years ago, yet civilization is much younger, around 6,000 BC.[51] The Genesis
account, which is clearly more than just myth, places Adam
and Eve in this more recent period and locates them in
exactly that part of the Middle East which scientists consider
the cradle of civilization. It was there that the 'hunter-gath-
erer' life-style changed to one of settled farming and allowed
the development of cities and working in metal, for instance
(Genesis 4:17,22).

Most conservative theologians, both Roman Catholic and
Protestant, believe that the whole human race descended
from that original pair. This would imply that all the primitive
men became extinct, as we know some did, for instance
Neanderthal man, and that God specially created Adam and
Eve. Others see Adam (the Hebrew word for *man*) and Eve
(Hebrew, *living*) as representing all the humans of their day,
Genesis itself indicating that there were others, such as those
already mentioned, among whom Cain went to live. For me,
this view fits better with what we know of early man. There
is evidence for instance, that *homo sapiens* lived in Australia
and America 10,000 years ago.[51]

The doctrine of original sin is discussed by Paul in Romans 5, where he says that sin entered the world through one man, Adam, and that as a result death came to us all. Whether or not Adam and Eve were the only human pair alive at the time, they acted representatively on behalf of all mankind. So as I see it, the doctrine of the fall of man does not require us to believe that a single human pair existed *as the only human beings* and we can regard Adam as the 'federal' head of humanity as Kidner suggests.[9]

Having said all that, I should in fairness add that Berry,[52] who is a professor of genetics, considers that *homo sapiens* passed through a population bottleneck in relatively recent times and is prepared to believe that God placed his image in just two pre-human creatures, who became Adam and Eve. This is his interpretation of Genesis 2:7: ' . . . God formed man from the dust of the ground . . . and man became a living soul'. However the word translated 'soul' in this quotation from the Authorized Version, is also used of animal life[9] and is translated 'being' in more recent versions. The verse is therefore not a description of pre-man suddenly getting a spiritual nature.

Is the Bible intended to convey modern science?

If we are to be true to the Bible, we have to decide whether the Genesis creation accounts are science in the modern sense. Are we taking liberties with the early chapters of Genesis, bending the meaning to fit the latest scientific fads? As I have tried to show in chapter 3, these sections of Genesis do not read like science. They have more important things to say. Yet the majestic creation narrative is not contradicted by modern science unless we read it as a literal history, and its simple grandeur makes the Babylonian and Assyrian records look quite grotesque by comparison. These records also mention a flood, but the area covered by this flood need not be the whole earth in the modern sense.[9] Whitcomb and

Morris[12] have assumed a universal flood during which the sedimentary rocks and fossils were laid down. Their arguments for an earth only a few thousand years old do not fit easily with what most see as clear, scientific evidence of an old earth.

As to the age of the earth, most scholars accept the six days of Genesis as six long spans of time. It is not easy to accept the account as scientific and each day as having an evening, a morning and a span of twenty-four hours since the sun is not created until day four (Genesis 1:16–19). The old editions of the Bible with BC 4004 printed over the first verse are relying on a calculation from the list of Adam's descendants in Genesis 5. As Kidner points out,[9] and even Whitcomb and Morris admit,[12] such genealogies need not represent an unbroken chain. Nor were the ancient Hebrews very precise about numbers, though it may well be that some of Noah's forbears lived very long lives.

Some creationists insist that there was no death or suffering in the world until Adam and Eve turned away from God. Along with this goes the view that the fall of man led to physical death.[11] If Adam and Eve were immortal, the mind boggles at the consequences of the instruction 'Be fruitful and increase in number' (Genesis 1:23) – an earth soon over-populated with their immortal descendants! As Berry points out,[52] the death that came to Adam as a result of the fall was spiritual, not physical, since he lived long after his expulsion from the Garden of Eden. When Paul says in 1 Corinthians 15 'as in Adam all die, so in Christ all will be made alive' he does not mean that Christians will live for ever in this world! The world of Genesis which God called good must have included pain and death if the living creatures described were anything like those we know today. (Some may argue of course that in two important ways the animals *were* unlike those we know today; that is they did not feel pain, nor did they die.)

To conclude then, science cannot discount the biblical

description of man as made in God's image. Though the first few chapters of Genesis are not scientific in the modern sense, they bear the marks of divine inspiration. As to their account of man's fall, we have only to read a history book or look in any newspaper. Gone are the days when biologists could believe in man's automatic moral progress from savage to savant. Two world wars have shown that the Bible gives us a truer description of human nature. And so it should, as the Maker's handbook!

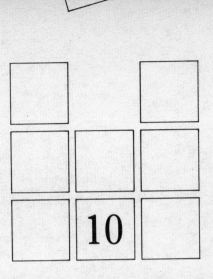

Clockwork humans?

10

Some years ago, my friend Donald MacKay wrote a book about science and Christian faith and called it *The Clockwork Image*.[24] The cover had a clockwork man on it, implying that in scientific terms we are just complicated machines, that what we call free choices are merely illusions and that any idea of a soul or spiritual nature is out of the question. These are the issues I want to face now but since so much has been said for and against evolutionary views of man's origin it might now be appropriate to sum up my personal views. There are plenty of others!

I take it then, that God has created the universe and all life and that the creation process involves his laws as they apply to the molecules from which we are made. The creation of life has been a long slow process culminating in the appearance of man. At some points it has seemed to enter blind alleys but the fact that we have arrived at the marvels of the human brain at all suggests that the God of history is in control. We cannot exclude the possibility of his 'special' intervention at certain points (*e.g.* the origin of life, the creation of man), but I prefer to think of the whole process as his special work. It will be objected that I am trying to have it both ways (evolution and creation) and that the blind alleys, suffering and death indicate a demon creator instead of a good God.[11] I am not unduly dismayed by this argument

'It's not working because it claims it can think and has decided not to.'

since the central affirmation of Christianity is that God's own son suffered and died.

Perhaps there is an analogy from God's dealings with the Jews. Abraham was chosen as the man whose descendants were to bring blessing to all nations (Genesis 12:3), a theme taken up by Peter in Acts 3:25 and Paul in Galatians 3:8. The New Testament writers see Jesus as the fulfilment of the promise to Abraham, since through him the whole world can know the forgiveness of God. Yet the journey from Abraham to Jesus is a sad and tortuous one. How often God's chosen people rebelled against him. Their whole history seems to be one of trouble and persecution. Yet they have survived as a nation – almost miraculously – and they have indeed been a blessing to the world, first in providing Jesus but also in providing countless fine scientists, artists, musicians and thinkers. Christians believe that the God of history has been in control all the time. From a human viewpoint it seems a strange way of doing things, but given human freedom and choice perhaps there was no other way. Though the Creator could have done otherwise, he seems to have decided that the best way of bringing life, and particularly human life, to this world was by a similar long, slow, painful process.

Human choice

Let me leave these unanaswerable questions and return to clockwork man. As Sidney Harris's cartoons are reminding you, computers seem to be taking over! No doubt you have heard the human brain described as a computer, albeit a pretty complicated one. If we knew enough about it, probably the brain could be *completely* described in terms of electrical circuits between its millions of nerve cells. So can we say that it is 'only a computer'?

This sort of 'nothing buttery' has been discussed in chapter 4 – and, I hope, dismissed. Humans can do a number of things that computers can't do, however complicated their programming. No doubt computers can do arithmetic faster than people can, but they are not able to make free choices and they can't fall in love! True, they can make choices if suitably programmed and these could either be logical or illogical. So if you knew the programme you could predict the choice. Human choices cannot be predicted in that way. Men and women quite often do things that don't make sense, that go against their whole previous upbringing and life-style. They are free agents. If not, the whole teaching of the Bible is at fault, because no-one can judge us, or forgive us, for that matter, if we are simply automata responding blindly to a mixture of programming and input from the environment.

A high class discussion of all this can be found in the book by Donald MacKay mentioned already[24] and for the more serious reader in his Henry Drummond lectures at the University of Stirling.[53] I think Donald would say, 'Of course we are machines – looked at from one point of view – but we are also persons'. If you prefer his own words: 'To make an "either-or" out of the choice between mechanistic and personal levels of human significance is now clearly fallacious. The question to be settled is only which level is appropriate to a given context, not which level you "believe in".'

My argument for human free-will would not convince a thorough-going behaviourist. Psychologists of this school say that freedom is an illusion, that all our choices are determined by our previous history and the external factors now acting upon us. A behaviourist would say that the people I spoke of who do things that go against their whole upbringing are really driven on by forces in the unconscious mind produced by some early experience in life. It is not easy to disprove such a theory and it is certainly possible to condition people by manipulating the environment. Authoritarian regimes of both the left and right use brain-washing for political purposes all too often.

There is a logical flaw in the extreme behaviourist view, however. If my thinking is the result of previous conditioning and outside irrational forces over which I have no control then it cannot represent truth. The same applies to the arguments of the behaviourist – they can all be explained away in terms of irrational influences, so why should I believe them?

The biologist J. B. S. Haldane, who certainly did not write as a Christian, made this point in another way:

> If my mental processes are determined solely by the motions of atoms in my brain, I have no reason to suppose that my beliefs are true ... hence I have no reason to suppose my brain to be composed of atoms.[54]

The soul

Which brings us to the old mind-body argument. The great seventeenth-century philosopher and scientist René Descartes believed that there was a dualism of mind and body. For him, the pineal gland of the brain was the site of interaction between the non-material soul and the material body. The ancient Greeks had the same idea of soul and body. Descartes had a simple proof of the reality of the soul: *cogito ergo sum* – 'I think, therefore I am'.

Some scientists today have similar views. Sir John Eccles, the neurophysiologist, considers that the mind interacts with the brain cortex, not the pineal, and that man's will can change the electrical circuits of the brain. He considers that this does not violate physical laws because the tiny energy changes are within the limits of the Heisenberg Uncertainty Principle (chapter 2, p. 19). Many scientists are unhappy about this particular idea, but the dualist view is certainly still alive. The philosopher Sir Karl Popper has collaborated with Eccles in a book on the subject.[55] Experimental support for the view comes from the work of Wilder Penfield, the

Canadian neurosurgeon. His work on surgical treatment of epilepsy led him to think that 'Something else finds its dwelling place between the sensory complex and the motor mechanism (the ability of the brain to cause body movements) . . . There is a switchboard operator was well as a switchboard'.

Other neuroscientists are 'monists' rather than dualists. They see no real evidence for the switchboard operator. For them the only reality is matter: 'mind' is a property of a complex system of brain cells, an 'epiphenomenon'.

MacKay[53] combines the dualist and monist views. He considers mental events as 'inside' aspects of brain events. The reality is so rich and complex that it has to be described in two ways, 'inside' and 'outside'.

The Bible's view

What does the Bible have to say about these questions? Contrary to popular belief, it does not support the idea of a 'soul' dwelling inside a physical body. As the discerning reader will have noticed already, words like mind and soul have been used quite loosely in the description of dualism above. I am afraid that Descartes was at fault there. For the Old Testament writers we are dust and to dust we shall return (Genesis 3:19), yet we have a special relationship to God. We are free agents made in his image (Genesis 1:27) and we are responsible beings who can be addressed by God. Man is a unity. His 'breath' or 'spirit' is not a separate entity, but the animating principle of the total person. The New Testament describes not the immortality of the soul but the resurrection of the total person – the 'spiritual body' of 1 Corinthians 15. Paul might seem to support dualism when he contrasts the 'flesh' and the 'spirit' in Romans 8 (Authorized Version), but modern translations make it clear that he meant our sinful nature or will when he used the word translated 'flesh'. He did not consider the body inherently evil and the soul good. Sin is in the will and Paul often writes of spritual sins such as pride.

The resurrection of the body takes us to the question of science and miracles, which is the next chapter. For the moment, let us sum up the 'clockwork humans' discussion. Both science and the Bible view man as a unity. Science cannot give us a satisfactory understanding of free-will or consciousness in physical terms, but their reality cannot be denied. MacKay sees no difficulty in principle with the idea of a conscious automaton, if we only knew enough to construct one! We use different words like mind, brain, personality, will and spirit to describe different aspects of the unity that is man but science provides no support for the concept that we are 'merely machines'. Though natural science (the old word was philosophy) has come a long way in the last few centuries it halts well before the things that matter most. Shakespeare knew as much: 'There are more things in heaven and earth, Horatio, than are dreamt of in your philosophy' (Hamlet Act I, Scene 5).

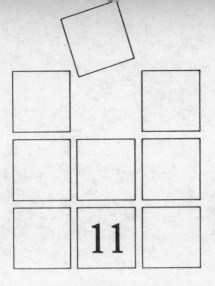

Miracles and prayer
in a mechanistic
world

11

Readers who have persisted so far, if there are any, will probably regard miracles as the crunch. In thinking about the origin of the universe, or of life, or mankind, perhaps there is room for a Creator. But miracles are just not on. We know that everything is subject to the laws of science, so we might as well believe in fairies or Father Christmas as in miracles. So runs the argument.

Even bishops have their doubts about miracles. One of them in the Anglican church, to which I belong, incidentally, made history in a fascinating way recently. Shortly before his consecration in York Minster he made statements which to the man in the pew, as it were, suggested disbelief in the virgin birth and resurrection of Jesus. Then shortly after the ceremony that noble Gothic building was struck by lightning. Was this a miracle – or at least a mark of divine disapproval? The letter writers to *The Times* had a field day. One quoted the chief fire officer of York as saying that 'the Lord was on our side as we battled with the flames' and wondered whom he had supported when the conflagration started. Another compared the episode with the 'fire from heaven' called down by Elijah, commenting that the fire in the Minster might be almighty fire threatening to burn down a cathedral in which 'recently there had been consecrated a bishop . . . who publicly expressed disbelief in several tenets of the Christian faith', only to be reminded by a later writer who knew his Bible better, that Elijah's fire did not indicate divine wrath. Nevertheless, for the Christian who believes in God's providence there are no such things as accidents. For those who will listen, perhaps there is a message in that fire at York Minster.

What has science to say then, about miracles? In the last analysis, only this: that they do not occur in the ordinary course of nature. Some people feel that science rules them 'out of court' as impossible events. Now some things are impossible in the sense of being self-contradictory – that two and two should make five or that a body should fail to move when impelled by an irresistible force, for instance. This is not the sort of possibility the scientific opponents of miracles have in mind, however. They say, rather, that the laws of science *forbid* miracles. But as we have seen, the laws of science do not cause, and therefore cannot forbid, anything. They are simply descriptions of what actually happens. If nature obeyed no such laws miracles would never be noticed. We are not saying that in miracles nature suddenly does things for no reason. Miracles are unusual events caused by God. The laws of nature are generalizations about usual events caused by God.

The scientist can only ask whether the records of the miracles are historically reliable. The answer is that we have better documents for them than for events like the Roman invasion of Britain which everyone accepts. One reason, incidentally, why some early documents such as the Apocryphal Gospels were excluded from the canon of Scripture was that they were full of rather pointless miracles. The miracles of the Bible are quite different. They show that God is interested in right and wrong, in healing the sick or feeding the hungry. They are neither propaganda nor magic.

Miracles in the Bible

Perhaps we should look at the Bible descriptions first. Not all miracles are of the same type. They are usually understood by the biblical writers as signs that God is working in a special way, interrupting the ordinary course of things. The great central miracle of Christianity, distinguishing it from all other religions, is the incarnation: 'The Word became flesh and lived for a while among us', says John's Gospel. Long before it happened, the Jewish prophet[56] wrote of a baby who would be called Immanuel, 'God with us'. Jesus made many references to his deity, even using the great Jewish expression for the self-existence of Jehovah and saying of himself 'before Abraham was born, I am!'.[57] In view of these statements, it is impossible to regard Jesus *merely* as a great teacher of morality. Yet many people, who do not know the Gospels very well, hold this view. As C. S. Lewis wrote:

A man who was merely a man and said the sort of things Jesus said wouldn't be a great moral teacher. He'd either be a lunatic – on a level with a man who says he's a poached egg – or else he'd be the Devil of Hell. You must make your choice. Either this man was, and is, the Son of God: or else a madman or something worse . . . But don't let us come with any patronizing nonsense about his being a great human teacher. He hasn't left that open to us. He didn't intend to.[58]

Granted this central fact, we should be prepared for miracles during Christ's earthly life. If this were God, the Author of all life, of course he would be able to heal the sick and raise the dead!

If we exclude the miracles of Jesus, most of the Bible miracles are connected with the young Christian church or with the prophets who led the Jews at various stages in their turbulent history. For some of these miracles the Bible itself supplies a natural explanation – one in terms of the forces usually at work in nature. In the crossing of the Red Sea (Sea of Reeds) for instance, a strong east wind is said to have driven back the waters.[59] The miraculous element here is in the timing. You could say that it was merely an amazing coincidence that the wind blew back the sea just as Moses and the Israelites arrived. The same might be said of Elijah's demonstration on Mount Carmel[60] mentioned already. It was rather fortunate that a thunderbolt or something like it came down and lit the altar fire just after Elijah had prayed for a demonstration of God's power.

The resurrection of Jesus

But there comes a point when it is easier to conclude that God answered the prayers of such men than that a series of fantastic 'coincidences' occurred. It is the same with so-called 'explanations' of the resurrection of Christ. We are told that he was not really dead, in spite of all the wounds he received and the hours on that terrible gallows. Or that his body was stolen, when the Jews had mounted a special guard to prevent that very thing. Or that those who saw the risen Jesus were having hallucinations, or mass hysteria in the case of the five hundred who saw him at once. It is easier to accept the fact that God raised his Son from the dead than to believe all the far-fetched 'explanations'. Without the resurrection, how can we explain the changed behaviour of the disciples? From being men hiding behind barred doors for fear of the Jews, they became preachers in the very synagogues themselves, men who 'turned the world upside down' (Acts 17:6, Authorized Version). The gospel or good news which they preached was mostly the resurrection of Jesus, as is clear from the early chapters of Acts. The Gospels we know were written later for those who had already accepted the good news about their Risen Lord. There would be no church today but for the resurrection.

The virgin birth

The virgin birth has attracted hostility, quite a lot of it from theologians. There is an interesting aside on it in Mark 6. The sceptical people of Nazareth say of Jesus, 'Isn't this the carpenter? Isn't this Mary's son? Perhaps Joseph had died by this time, but even so, referring only to the mother was unusual and suggested illegitimacy. It is not impossible that when the Jews of Jerusalem say to Jesus, 'We are not illegitimate children' (John 8:41) they are referring obliquely to the gossip about his birth.

Matthew records the reaction of Joseph to the news that his fiancée is pregnant. He draws the obvious conclusion and prepares to divorce Mary quietly, as the Jewish law allowed (Deuteronomy 24:1) but is then told in a dream that there has been no unfaithfulness. On the contrary, Mary's conception is from the Holy Spirit and the child is to be called Jesus because he will save his people from their sins. A similar angelic messenger has explained the promised birth to Mary and her side of the story is told by Luke: 'How will this be', Mary asks the angel, 'since I am a virgin?' (Luke 1:34). The answer is the same: 'The Holy Spirit will come upon you, and the power of the Most High will overshadow you'.

C. S. Lewis[20] comments that no human father creates his child, he merely provides a microscopic spermatozoon, 'behind which lies the whole history of the universe'. The DNA it contains has a genetic message which goes back to the first germ of life and has reached man through millions of ancestors. But that line of ancestors is in God's hand, says Lewis:

It is the instrument by which He normally creates a

man ... But once, and for a special purpose, He dispensed with that long line which is His instrument: once His life-giving finger touched a woman without passing through the ages of interlocked events. Once the great glove of Nature was taken off His hand. His naked hand touched her.

You might think that this was one of the easier miracles since virgin birth (parthenogenesis) – or the development of an unfertilized ovum into an adult – is known to insect biologists. That was not the explanation however, or Jesus would have had only his mother's chromosomes and been a girl!

Scofield[8] also has an interesting comment about the virgin birth. There are two genealogies of Jesus in the gospels, one in Luke 3 and the other in Matthew 1. Though they both refer to Jesus as son of Joseph, it seems that Luke gives the ancestry of Mary which differs from that of Joseph. She is descended from King David through his son Nathan, while Joseph's line runs from Solomon. This line includes Jeconiah (Matthew 1:11), also called Coniah, and, in the New International Version, Jehoiachin, and referred to by the prophet Jeremiah (22:24–30), who predicted that none of Jeconiah's descendants would occupy the throne of David. Since Jesus in a sense is to occupy the throne of David (Luke 1:32) this prophecy would be contradicted if Joseph had been the true father of Jesus. So in this obscure prophecy we have independent confirmation of the virgin birth.

We are prone to say the miracles could not have occurred merely because we are not used to them! This proves nothing. There is a sense in which everything is incredible. It is amazing that trees should burst into leaf once a year, or that the earth should spin in empty space, or that one small cell should grow into a man. We stop marvelling because we are used to it all. Someone from a world where such things were unknown might be excused if he said 'impossible'.

Scientists draw tremendous conclusions about the universe from studies on one small speck of it, our little earth. Reality may be much stranger than we can imagine, locked in our narrow world of space and time. If we knew more, perhaps we should understand that the miracles were not just exceptions to the normal laws of science but essential threads in a fabric of events too large for us now to see.

Can God answer prayer?

If we can accept miracles, can we accept the Christian view that God can answer prayer? Much the same problem faces us. If the universe is a sort of mechanism, running according to fixed laws, it seems quite improper for even its Creator to tinker with it in response to human requests. Yet the teaching of Jesus is quite plain: 'Ask and it will be given to you; seek and you will find' (Matthew 7:7).

Prayer presents various difficulties. For instance, who are we to ask an all-wise and all-knowing God to do something? He knows best and will do what is best without prompting or advice from us. This is not the place to discuss such problems, and in any case my simple answer could be to do what Jesus says. Even those who cannot accept him as Son of God must see his wisdom and the authority of his moral teaching – the authority of one short life which has influenced the world for good more than any other.

Prayer would indeed be futile if we lived in a closed mechanistic universe. But science makes no such claim. It certainly finds regularity and order (the laws of science) but eminent philosophers of science such as Whitehead or Popper see the universe as flexible and open, having novelty as well as regularity.

Most of the things we pray about are unpredictable – the result of an operation, or an interview for a job. As C. S. Lewis pointed out,[61] we don't pray about eclipses. So it is only our ignorance that makes petitionary prayers possible.

Surely, says the agnostic, science will predict the future once we know enough about the way everything works. Setting aside the unpredictability of people, will science ever do that? With Lewis, I doubt it. No one sunrise has ever been like another. Behind every physical event lies the whole history of the universe; each event is really unique. The God of history weaves what we call the future from such events, but also from our contributions, prayer included. Science makes neither prayer nor miracles unacceptable.

One question remains as we turn back to miracles. Are they just capricious examples of God's power or part of some long-term plan? The Bible suggests that they are essential parts of the plan to save humanity from evil. God's chosen people were to keep pure the knowledge of Jehovah until 'in the fullness of time' his own Son should be born into their race and eventually 'slain for the sins of the world'. A strange remedy for the world's ills, to human ears! Yet the message of this gospel, accepted by individual men and women, has made changes in hearts and lives which are often miraculous too.

12

Brave new world

12

Are we on the way to Utopia? Until two world wars and the atom bomb sapped their confidence, people used to talk about human progress. We had risen from savages and a suitable mixture of education and sanitation would eventually produce a perfect race of men.

The Bible says little about progress. In fact it suggests that the world will end in a mess and that there will have to be a new heaven and a new earth. 'Just about typical', says the agnostic reader. 'I'll be generous and grant that there is no basic conflict between science and the Bible, but frankly, I'd rather it did talk about progress. Does the Christain faith have anything useful to say about the human condition? I'm not absolutely sold on science either, come to that. Convince me that there's a better way'.

Let's go back to progress. In one way we have certainly progressed. Since primitive man learned that flint chipped in the right way gave him a cutting edge, the march of technology has continued. Our trouble is that we attach such importance to it. Bernard Levin gets the persepctive: 'We have long since ceased to put our trust in the princes who wear coronets, but we now rely instead, and no less blindly, on those which wear winking lights and give off a low hum when their buttons are pressed'.

Yet each new technique provides a new problem. If my

113

'We programmed it to simulate living conditions in the year 2000, and it's become hysterical.'

neighbour has a grudge against me, I'd rather he arrived with an old bone or a wooden club than with a hand grenade. And a burglar with a Ph.D. in engineering science can give my house a miss. Early man may or may not have been aggressive, but at least he could not turn the world into a radioactive graveyard.

So must we get rid of science, take to the hills as some young idealists have done, bake our own bread and return to nature? Even if it were possible for everyone, it would do no good. Our problems would go with us. The fault lies not in our technology but in ourselves.

Some of us have picked up a vague cynicism about Christianity from our elders at school or college. Others are just ignorant of its real meaning. Relatively few of us take the trouble to look at the evidence for ourselves, which would be the scientific thing to do. There is no shortage of books about the Christian faith, written from every possible viewpoint (some of them begging every possible question too!). Best of all, there is the Bible itself, perhaps John's Gospel to begin with.

An honest reader of that Gospel must conclude that it is either a beautiful fairy story or the most tremendous news the world can offer. It is a solemn decision. What is the tremendous news then? Briefly that God's own Son died on a common gallows so that all men and women might be forgiven and live for ever.

The idea that we need to repent, to be forgiven, is foreign to us in this scientific age. Psychiatrists talk of guilt complexes and certainly there is unhealthy guilt. There is also real guilt. We can see, even as we excuse our own faults, that friends and relatives *ought* to feel guilty. Yet selfishness lives in every heart and given favourable conditions will grow into the things which fill our newspapers with such depressing reading. The Bible's message is that only almighty God can deliver us from this and make new men and women of us.

115

Can science make us better people?

Science and technology have made life both more comfortable and more terrible. In a world hungry for energy should we use nuclear power stations or is the anti-nuclear movement right, 'better active today than radioactive tomorrow'? An American company is offering frozen human sperm to European doctors by mail order. What control should there be over artificial insemination by donor? Techniques of genetic engineering may allow us one day to cure diseases which cannot now be treated. What if it also becomes possible to clone humans? Erwin Chargaff, one of the pioneers of DNA biochemistry, is not too happy about 'human engineering':

> Once you can alter the chromosomes at will, you will be able to tailor the average Consumer, the predictable user of a given soap, the reliable imbiber of a certain poison gas. You will have given humanity a present compared with which the Hiroshima bomb was a friendly easter egg. You will indeed have touched the ecology of death. I shudder to think in whose image this new man will be made.[62]

What a brave new world science can give us! Yet if more science is not the answer to our problems, more money will not work either. Keeping inflation in single figures will not cure everything in a world where more than half the inhabitants are starving and a good many of the others are overfed. Come to that, getting them all fed will not cure everything either. Crimes of violence are not notably less common in the richest countries. All political systems, all decisions about the use of new technology, finally depend on people. Good people or bad people. People interested in their own comfort, their own power, their own appetites; or people willing to love God and their fellows more than anything else. Political systems, however just, will not cure the world of sin. Complicated ethical codes or legal systems are likewise powerless. Only a new quality of life will do.

Jesus said to Nicodemus, a clever man and a deeply religious one, 'You must be born again' (John 3:7). Summarizing the facts about Christ, a New Testament letter says: 'God has given us eternal life, and this life is in his Son. He who has the Son has life; he who does not have the Son of God does not have life' (1 John 5:11–12).

Appropriately, the only way to check the truth of this is the scientific one. We need to make the experiment, to put our trust in the Person so clearly portrayed in the Gospel accounts. Sometimes learning may be a hindrance, whether scientific or not. Peter, in his simple, down-to-earth way, came to the heart of the matter: 'Lord, to whom shall we go? You have the words of eternal life' (John 6:68).

References

1 A. D. White, *A History of the Warfare of Science with Theology* (1896. Republished 1960 by Dover Publications, New York). White had been involved in another, worthier struggle, to free universities and colleges from domination by the clergy. His was the era of the 'non-sectarian' colleges in the U.S.A. In his youth Oxford and Cambridge were entirely under ecclesiastical control but by the end of the century holy orders had become a handicap rather than an advantage to those seeking a university post there.

2 Genesis 1:28 (Authorized Version or New International Version) Professor R. Hooykaas in *Religion and the Rise of Modern Science*, (Scottish Academic Press, Edinburgh, 1973) has given a full account of the evidence that experimental science has its roots in the Jewish-Christian view of nature.

3 E. F. Schumacher, *A Guide for the Perplexed* (Jonathan Cape, London, 1977).

4 Karl Popper, *Objective Knowledge* (Oxford University Press, 1972).

5 J. C. Polkinghorne, *The Particle Play* (W. H. Freeman, Oxford and San Francisco, 1979). Supposed to be non-technical, but it's not a book for those who are scared of mathematics.

6 J. C. Polkinghorne, *The Way The World Is* subtitled 'The Christian perspective of a scientist' (Triangle, SPCK London) John Polkinghorne FRS was Professor of Mathematical Physics in Cambridge until 1979. He is now an Anglican priest.

7 A chapter on the space sciences by R. L. F. Boyd in *Horizons of Science* edited by Carl F. H. Henry (Harper & Row, San Francisco, 1977).

8 C. T. Scofield. ed., *New Scofield Reference Bible* (Oxford University Press, New York, 1967). The comments on prophecy run as follows: 'Fulfilled prophecy is a proof of inspiration because the Scripture predictions of future events were uttered so long before the events took place that no mere human sagacity or foresight could have anticipated them, and these predictions are so detailed, minute and specific as to exclude the possibility that they were simply fortunate guesses'. Who would have expected the Messiah's birth at a small town so far off the beaten track as Bethlehem, for instance? Or the return of the Jews to their own state of Israel in our own century? Scofield continues: 'Hundreds of predictions concerning Israel, the land of Canaan, Babylon, Assyria, Egypt, and numerous personages – so ancient, so singular, so seemingly improbable,. . . . have been fulfilled by the elements and by men who were ignorant of them, or who utterly disbelieved them, or who struggled with frantic desperation to avoid their fulfillment. It is certain therefore, that the Scriptures which contain them are inspired'.

9 Derek Kidner, *Genesis*, (Tyndale Old Testament Commentary, I.V.P., London, 1967.) This commentary gives a balanced account of some of the scientific problems without dishonour to biblical authority.

10 Feminists will understand, I hope, that 'man' is used here in the biological sense to mean both sexes. It would be merely tedious to say 'man and woman', 'he and she' every time. As the biology teacher unwittingly remarked,

man embraces woman.

11 N. M. de S. Cameron, *Evolution and the Authority of the Bible* (Paternoster Press, Exeter, 1983).

12 J. C. Whitcomb Jr. & H. M. Morris, *The Genesis Flood*, (Baker Book House, Grand Rapids, Michigan, 1974, 18th impression).

13 In Matthew 19:4–6 Jesus is quoting Genesis 1:27 and 2:24. Interestingly, he does not refer specifically to Adam and Eve, but only to God making them 'male and female' in the beginning.

14 H. Blocher, *In the beginning* (I.V.P., Leicester, 1984).

15 Romans 5:12–21; I Corinthians 15: 35–49.

16 Derek Kidner, *Genesis*, p.29.

17 John Stott, *The Bible: Book for Today* (I.V.P., Leicester, 1982).

18 For instance Edwin M. Yamauchi, *The Stones and the Scriptures*, (I.V.P., London, 1973).

19 John 7:17.

20 C. S. Lewis, *Miracles*, first published in 1947, now available in Fontana paperback (Collins, London and Glasgow).

21 Shakespeare's *Hamlet*, Act V, Scene 2; based on Matthew 10:29.

22 Acts 17:27–28. More fully, the poem says of the Supreme God: 'But Thou are not dead; for ever Thou art risen and alive, For in Thee we live and move and have our being'.

23 R. Hooykaas, *Religion and the Rise of Modern Science* (Scottish Academic Press, Edinburgh, 1973).

24 Donald MacKay, *The Clockwork Image* (I.V.P., London, 1974).

25 Genesis 3:19 and 1:26.

26 John Polkinghorne, in *The Way the World Is* (see reference 6) quotes a common view: 'It seems that the only role left for God is the deistic one of lighting the blue touch-paper to set off the big bang, and then retiring'. As the

book develops of course, Polkinghorne finds more for God to do!

27 John 14:6 (New International Version) – in full, 'I am the way and the truth and the life'.

28 F. Hoyle, *The Nature of the Universe* (Blackwell, Oxford, 1950).

29 K. R. Popper in *Studies on the Philosophy of Biology*, edited by F. J. Ayala and T. Dobzhansky (Macmillan, London, 1974).

30 F. Hoyle and C. Wickramasinghe, *Evolution from Space* (J. M. Dent and Sons, London, 1981).

31 F. Crick, *Life Itself: Its Origin and Nature* (Macdonald, London and Sydney, 1981).

32 Sir Thomas Browne, *Religio Medici and other works*, edited by L. C. Martin (Oxford University Press, 1964).

33 Psalm 139:13–16 (New International Version).

34 C. Darwin, *The Origin of Species* (1st edition reprinted with editor's introduction and historical sketch by Darwin, Penguin Books, Harmondsworth, 1968).

35 C. Patterson, *Evolution* (Routledge and Kegan Paul, London, 1978).

36 L. Bounoure, *Recherche d'une doctrine de la vie*, (Laffont, Paris, 1964).

37 P.-P. Grasse, *Evolution of Living Organisms: Evidence for a New Theory of Transformation* (Academic Press, New York, 1977).

38 G. A. Kerkut, *Implications of Evolution* (Pergamon Press, Oxford, 1960).

39 D. Dewar, *The Transformist Illusion* (De Hoff Publications, Murfreesboro, Tennessee, 1957).

40 E. B. Chain, 'Social Responsibility and the Scientist', *Perspectives in Biology and Medicine*, 14 (1971), 347.

41 *Father and Son, a Study of Two Temperaments* by Edmund Gosse (Oxford University Press, London, 1974) is a classic in which Edmund describes life with his father Philip. *Omphalos* by P. H. Gosse F.R.S. (John van Voorst,

London, 1857) is now difficult to obtain, though university libraries will be able to borrow copies using the interlibrary loan scheme.

42 R. Duncan and M. Weston-Smith (editors), *The Encyclopaedia of Ignorance* (Pergamon Press, Oxford, 1977).

43 G. R. Taylor, *The Great Evolution Mystery* (Secker and Warburg, London, 1983).

44 M. Ruse, *Darwinism Defended* (Addison-Wesley, Reading, Mass., 1982).

45 A. Hayward, *God Is* (Marshall, Morgan and Scott, London, 1978).

46 I. G. Barbour, *Issues in Science and Religion* (SCM Press, London, 1968).

47 S. J. Gould, *Ever Since Darwin* (Burnett & Andre Deutsch, London, 1978).

48 E. O. Wilson, *Sociobiology: the New Synthesis* (Harvard University Press, Cambridge, Mass., 1975).

49 K. Bock, *Human Nature and History: a response to sociobiology* (Columbia University Press, New York, 1980).

50 D. Lack, *Evolutionary Theory and Christian Belief* (Methuen, London, 1961).

51 G. A. Harrison, J. S. Weiner, J. M. Tanner, N. A. Barnicot and V. Reynolds, *Human Biology*, 2nd edition (Oxford University Press, 1977).

52 R. J. Berry, *Adam and the Ape* (Falcon Books, CPAS, London, 1975).

53 D. M. MacKay, *Brains, Machines and Persons* (Collins, London, 1980).

54 J. B. S. Haldane, *Possible Worlds* (Chatto and Windus, London, 1930).

55 K. R. Popper and J. Eccles, *The Self and Its Brain* (Springer Verlag, New York, 1977). For a brief outline of the Popper-Eccles argument and other useful information, see A. C. Custance, *The Mysterious Matter of Mind* (Zondervan Publishing House, Grand Rapids, Michigan, 1980).

56 Isaiah 7:14.

57 John 8:58 (New International Version).

58 C. S. Lewis, *Broadcast Talks* (Geoffrey Bles, London, 1942).

59 Exodus 14:21.

60 I Kings 18.

61 *C. S. Lewis, Letters to Malcolm, chiefly on Prayer* (Geoffrey Bles, London, 1964).

62 E. Chargaff, 'Voices in the Labyrinth: Dialogues Around the Study of Nature', (*Perspectives in Biology and Medicine*, 18, 1975, 251).

For further reading

These suggestions are for those who want to read the subject more deeply and see more than one point of view. I have added my own reactions to each one, but you will not necessarily agree!

C. S. Lewis, in my opinion the greatest Christian apologist of this century, was neither a theologian nor a scientist. All his books are worth reading, if only for their splendid English style. In particular, *Miracles* (paperback by Fontana, 1960) discusses many of the topics considered here and *That Hideous Strength* (as Lewis puts it 'a tall story about devilry') is exciting science fiction dealing with the ruthless exploitation of a biological discovery. It is also published in paperback (Pan Books, 1983).

Colin Russell is Professor of History of Science and Technology at the Open University and his book *Cross-currents: interactions between science and faith* (Inter-Varsity Press, 1985) deals with the history of science and its interaction with Christianity. Readable and a good source book for even more reading.

Also on the general subject of science and faith, but from different Christian backgrounds, are the following four books: *The Way The World Is* (paperback, Triangle, SPCK, 1983) was written by John Polkinghorne FRS, a Cambridge Professor of Mathematical Physics who resigned in 1979 to become an Anglican clergyman. *Creation and the World of Science* (Oxford University Press, 1979) by A. R. Peacocke, is wide-ranging and scholarly, as would be expected from a Dean of Clare College Cambridge who is also a physical biochemist. A more popular book by Alan Hayward shows why it makes sense for a scientist to believe in God – or at least that is what the dust-jacket claims. I found it helpful (*God Is*, Marshall, Morgan and Scott, 1978). A modern attempt at natural theology (getting to God from nature, though possibly not the God of the Bible) is by the Bishop of Birmingham. It is called, modestly enough, *The Probability of God* (Hugh Montefiore, S.C.M. Press, 1985). According to the Introduction, the Bishop's wife checked the manuscript for its intelligibility to non-scientists, but I found it hard going.

The remaining books concentrate on creation and evolution. *The Great Brain Robbery* is a lively paperback which calls evolution an ancient Greek philosophy masquerading as modern science (David C. C. Watson, Henry Walter, 1975). Also highly critical of evolution is *From Nothing to Nature*, Evangelical Press, 1978. The author, Professor E. H. Andrews, is a physicist rather than a biologist and the book is written for teenagers. A more moderate criticism of evolutionary theory is provided by Alan Hayward (*Creation and Evolution: the Facts and fallacies*, Triangle, SPCK, 1985, London), though I found this a heavier book to read than *God Is*. The author would not agree with the creationists who insist on a young earth. *Darwinism Defended* (Addison-Wesley, 1982, Reading, Mass., U.S.A.) by Michael Ruse, a Canadian professor who is an expert on the history and philosophy of biology, is what it says, an unashamed defence of Darwin against what Ruse calls the lunatic ideas of the American 'creation scientists'. It is not particularly Christian.

Finally, *Creation and Evolution*, edited by Derek Burke, gives both sides of the debate. It is part of a series called *When Christians disagree* (Inter-Varsity Press, 1985) and I found it very good. This may be because Derek Burke is an old friend who was Professor of Biochemistry in Warwick University before going to Canada, but as far as I know it is the only book dealing with evolution and Christian views of creation which mentions the recent evidence from molecular biology. All the others are still in the fossil era and need to catch up. It will not have escaped you that I have tried to deal with the molecular biology! *Evolution and the Authority of the Bible* by Nigel M. de S. Cameron (Paternoster Press, 1983), which is firmly against evolution, does have an appendix on DNA, but oddly leaves out the molecular biology which relates to evolution.

Index

WHO

KILLED

CHRISTOPHER

GOODMAN?